AF526508

The Mahabharata in Rhyme

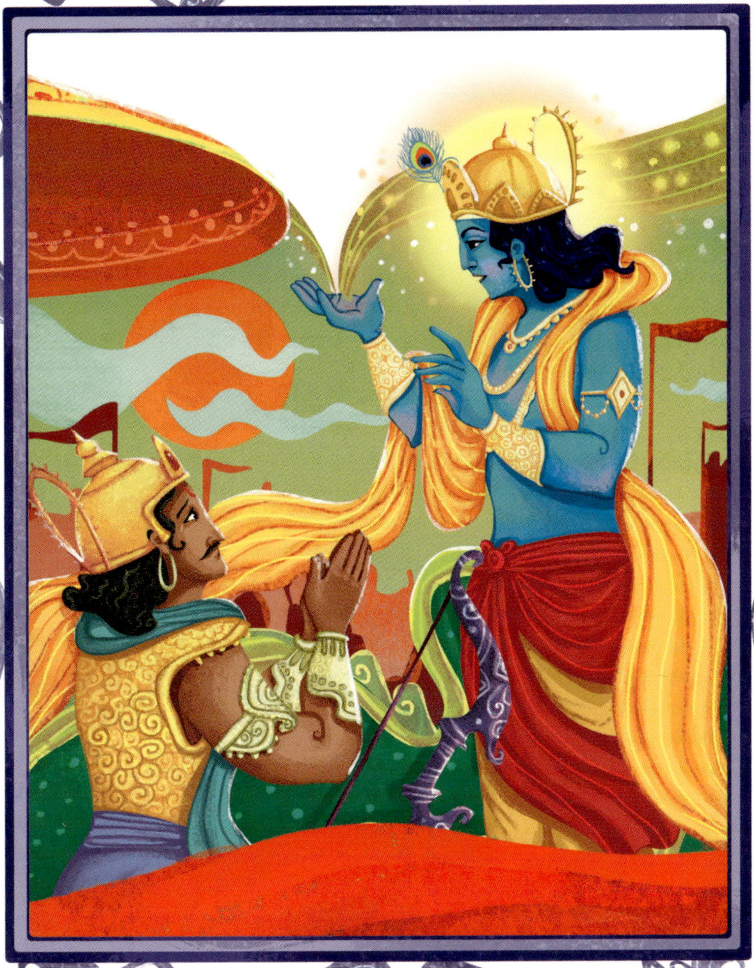

Retold by

Sia Gupta

First published in 2021 by

Om Kidz | Om Books International

Corporate & Editorial Offic
A-12, Sector 64, Noida 201 301
Uttar Pradesh, India
Phone: +91 120 477 4100
Email: editorial@ombooks.com
Website: www.ombooksinternational.com

Sales Office
107, Ansari Road, Darya Ganj
New Delhi 110 002, India
Phone: +91 11 4000 9000
Email: sales@ombooks.com

Author: Sia Gupta
Editor: Kirti Pathak
Art & Design: Anshuman Pandey, Savita kundal, Harish Arya

ISBN: 9789353767310

Printed in India

10 9 8 7 6 5 4 3 2 1

Contents

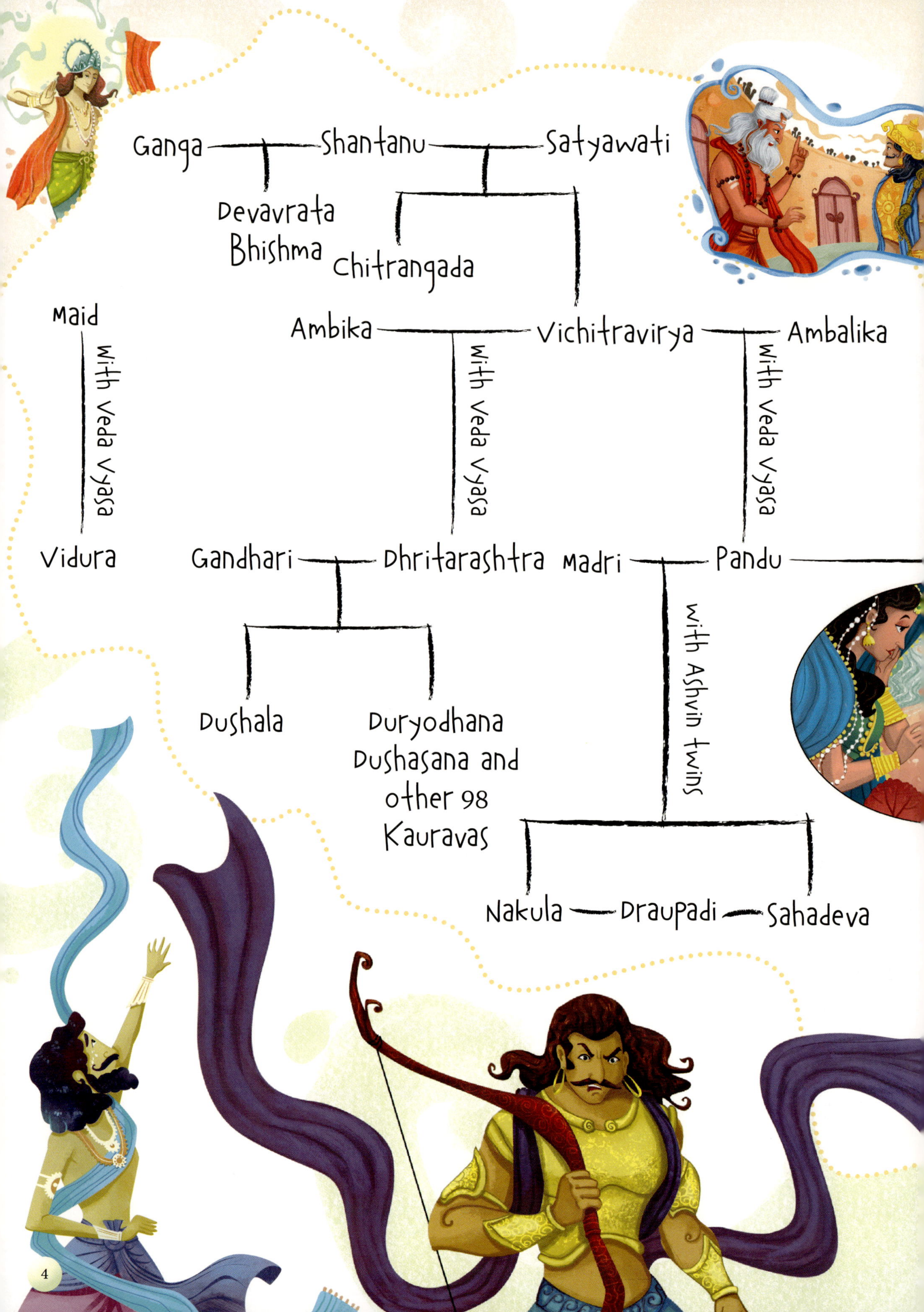
Ganga
Shantanu
Satyawati
Devavrata
Bhishma
Chitrangada
Maid
Ambika
Vichitravirya
Ambalika
with Veda Vyasa
with Veda Vyasa
with Veda Vyasa
Vidura
Gandhari
Dhritarashtra
Madri
Pandu
with Ashvin twins
Dushala
Duryodhana
Dushasana and
other 98
Kauravas
Nakula
Draupadi
Sahadeva

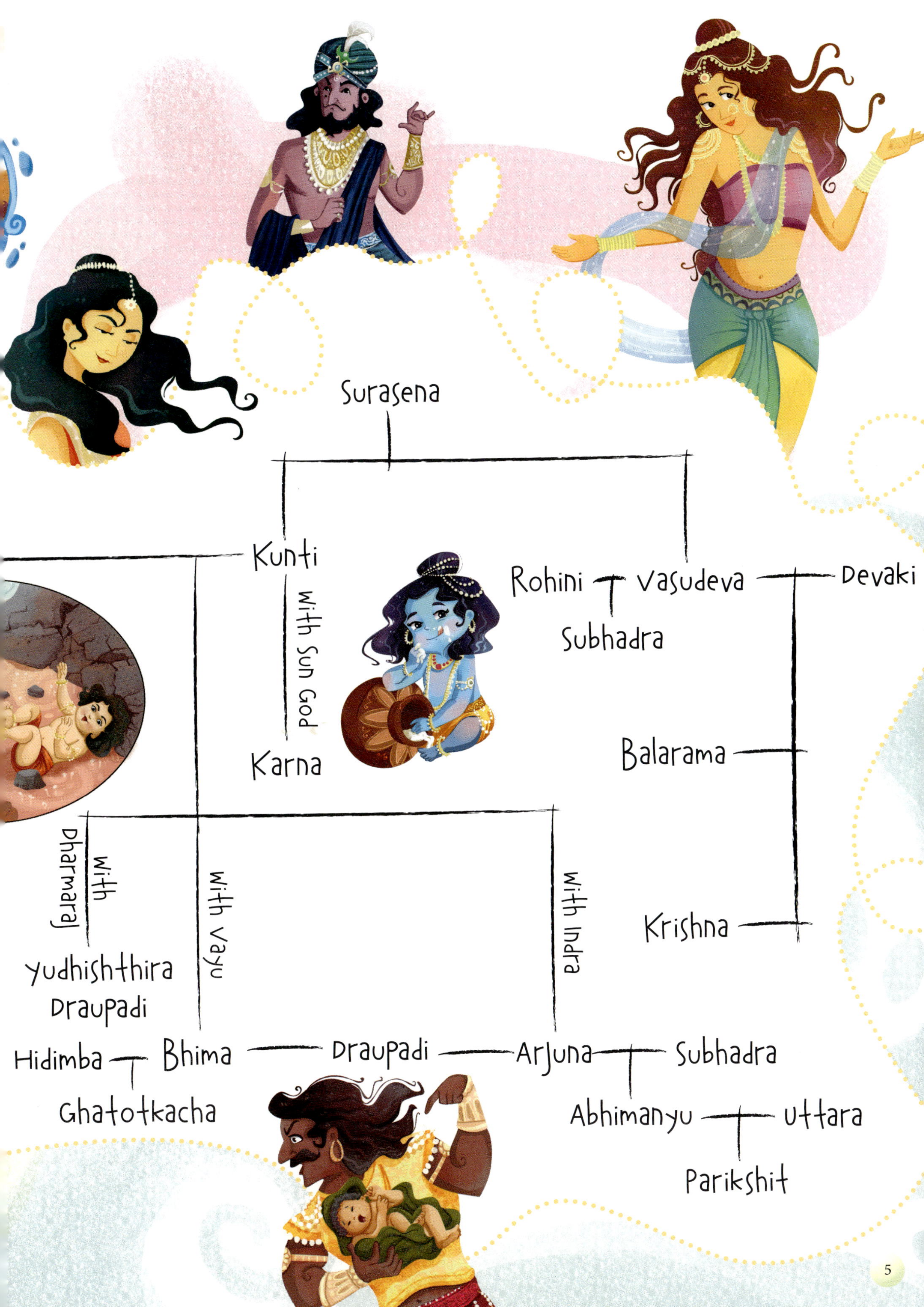
Surasena
Kunti
with Sun God
Karna
Rohini
Vasudeva
Devaki
Subhadra
Balarama
Krishna
with Dharmaraj
Yudhishthira
Draupadi
with Vayu
with Indra
Hidimba
Bhima
Draupadi
Arjuna
Subhadra
Ghatotkacha
Abhimanyu
Uttara
Parikshit

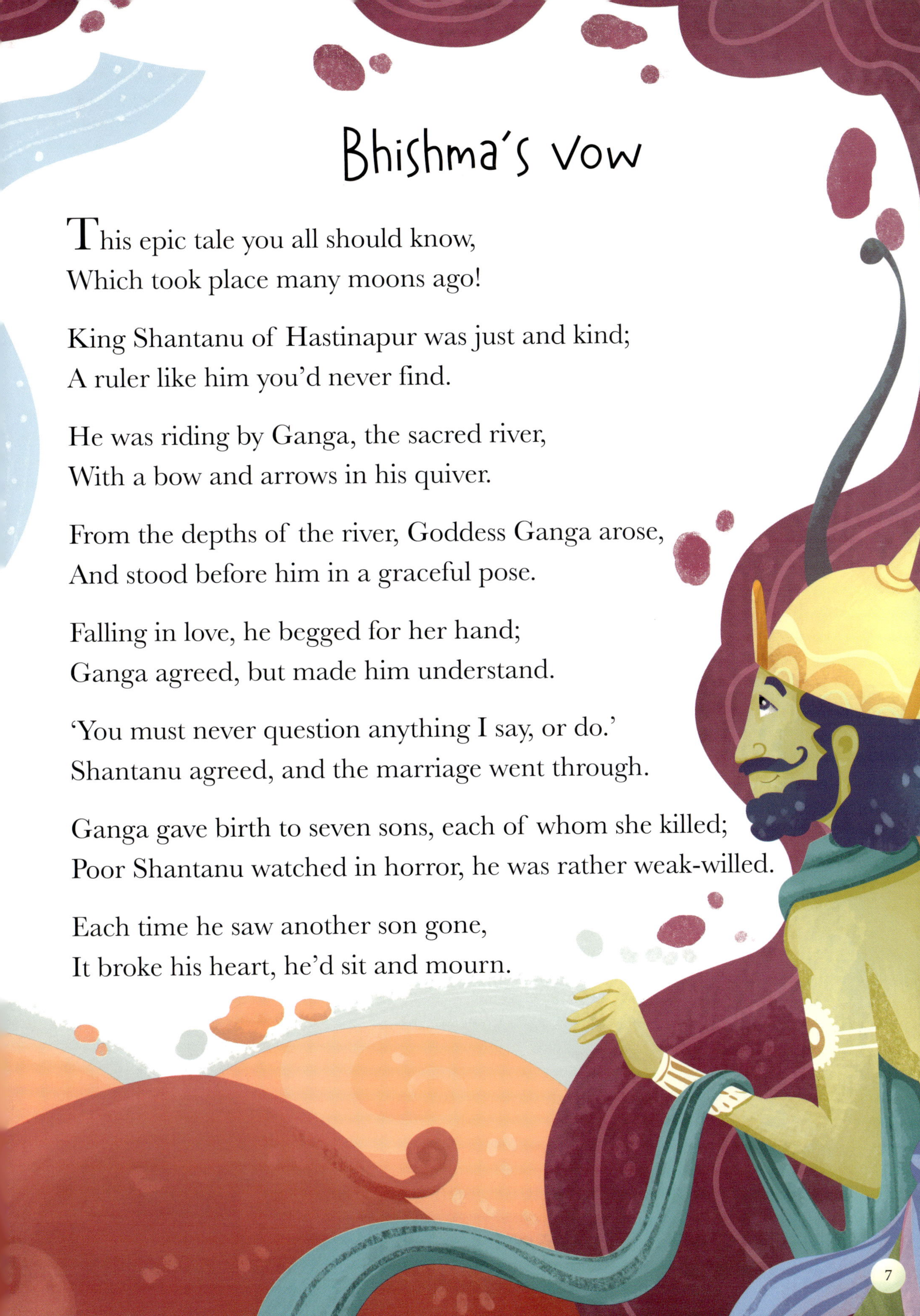

Bhishma's vow

This epic tale you all should know,
Which took place many moons ago!

King Shantanu of Hastinapur was just and kind;
A ruler like him you'd never find.

He was riding by Ganga, the sacred river,
With a bow and arrows in his quiver.

From the depths of the river, Goddess Ganga arose,
And stood before him in a graceful pose.

Falling in love, he begged for her hand;
Ganga agreed, but made him understand.

'You must never question anything I say, or do.'
Shantanu agreed, and the marriage went through.

Ganga gave birth to seven sons, each of whom she killed;
Poor Shantanu watched in horror, he was rather weak-willed.

Each time he saw another son gone,
It broke his heart, he'd sit and mourn.

By the eighth child, he could bear it no longer;
He realised he'd have to be much stronger.

He firmly stopped Ganga and said,
'Don't put this child on his death bed.

What kind of mother would kill her own child?
No one does this, not even someone wild.'

Then Ganga revealed that it was a curse;
Had those children lived on, it'd be far worse.

Saying, 'This child is blessed with a boon,'
She took him; with a promise to return him soon.

Every day, Shantanu would wait and see
If Ganga had finally set his eighth son free.

When at last she sent their child,
The proud Shantanu then joyfully smiled.

Devavrata, his son, now a young man of sixteen
Was the best warrior the world had ever seen.

Shantanu thought, *As king, he shall be fair and just;*
My warrior son they all shall trust!

Amid great rejoicing, he was crowned;
The heir to Hastinapur had been found.

But Shantanu pined for his beloved queen;
He remembered how joyful the days with Ganga had been.

He wanted another wife, who was beautiful and fair;
He searched in vain here, there, everywhere!

One day, he decided to go hunting with his son.
Now the story becomes an interesting one!

In their carriages, Shantanu and Devavrata rode
Through the most bumpy and difficult road.

Devavrata continued, but Shantanu stopped
At the riverbank, and his eyes almost popped!

When he saw Satyawati, a beautiful maid,
Shantanu was smitten, and for her he craved.

'I wish to marry you,' he said;
Satyawati agreed, and her cheeks turned red!

He went to her father to seek her hand,
Who was a cunning and greedy fellow of the land.

He agreed, but said in a serious tone,
'Satyawati's son must inherit the throne.'

The king thought, *But Devavrata is the rightful heir!*
Disappointed and distracted, he left from there.

Devavrata was worried at his father's plight;
He went to investigate to set things right.

When he learnt about Satyawati, and her father's condition,
He asked him to reconsider his decision.

Her father repeated what he'd told Shantanu;
Devavrata was angered, and saddened too!

For his father's sake he abdicated the throne;
He couldn't bear to see his father so sad and alone.

He vowed that Satyawati's son would rule the land,
By whose side he, himself, would always stand.

Satyawati's father was not happy with just that;
He said in a cunning tone which was low and flat.

'What if your children claim the throne and fight?
Your vow doesn't take away their right.'

Then Devavrata took a vow he would forever carry;
He declared that he would never, ever marry!

The gods from above showered flowers at his feet;
Devavrata became Bhishma for the vow that none could repeat.

When the villagers found out, they were full of rage;
To pacify them, Bhishma declared from the stage,

'I vow to see my father's image in every king;
And prosperity to this state, I promise to bring.

I will not rest until Hastinapur is safe and sound,
For my kingdom's well-being, I'll always be around.'

Goddess Ganga arose from the water then;
She said, 'Bhishma will be a God amongst men.

He won't die even when he's old and tired;
He'll die only when he himself desired.'

Bhishma accepted the boon with humility and grace,
Regardless of what all in life he'd have to face.

Shantanu and Satyawati became husband and wife,
But life in Hastinapur would be full of strife.

Amba Vows Revenge against Bhishma

Satyawati had Chitrangada and Vichitravirya as two sons;
Shantanu's death left her taking care of these young ones.

Chitrangada was crowned king, but when he died,
Vichitravirya ascended the throne with no queen by his side.

Meanwhile in Kashi, the kingdom ruled by Kashya, the King,
Preparations for a wedding were on in full swing.

Princesses Amba, Ambika and Ambalika were soon to marry;
The family tradition of marrying princes they were obliged to carry.

All the kingdoms, except Hastinapur, were invited;
Bhishma took offence and was hasty and short-sighted.

Vichitravirya shall marry the princesses, he decided;
To Satyawati, his grand plan he then confided.

Bhishma rode to Kashi on his chariot and horse;
He was stronger than the mightiest, full of force.

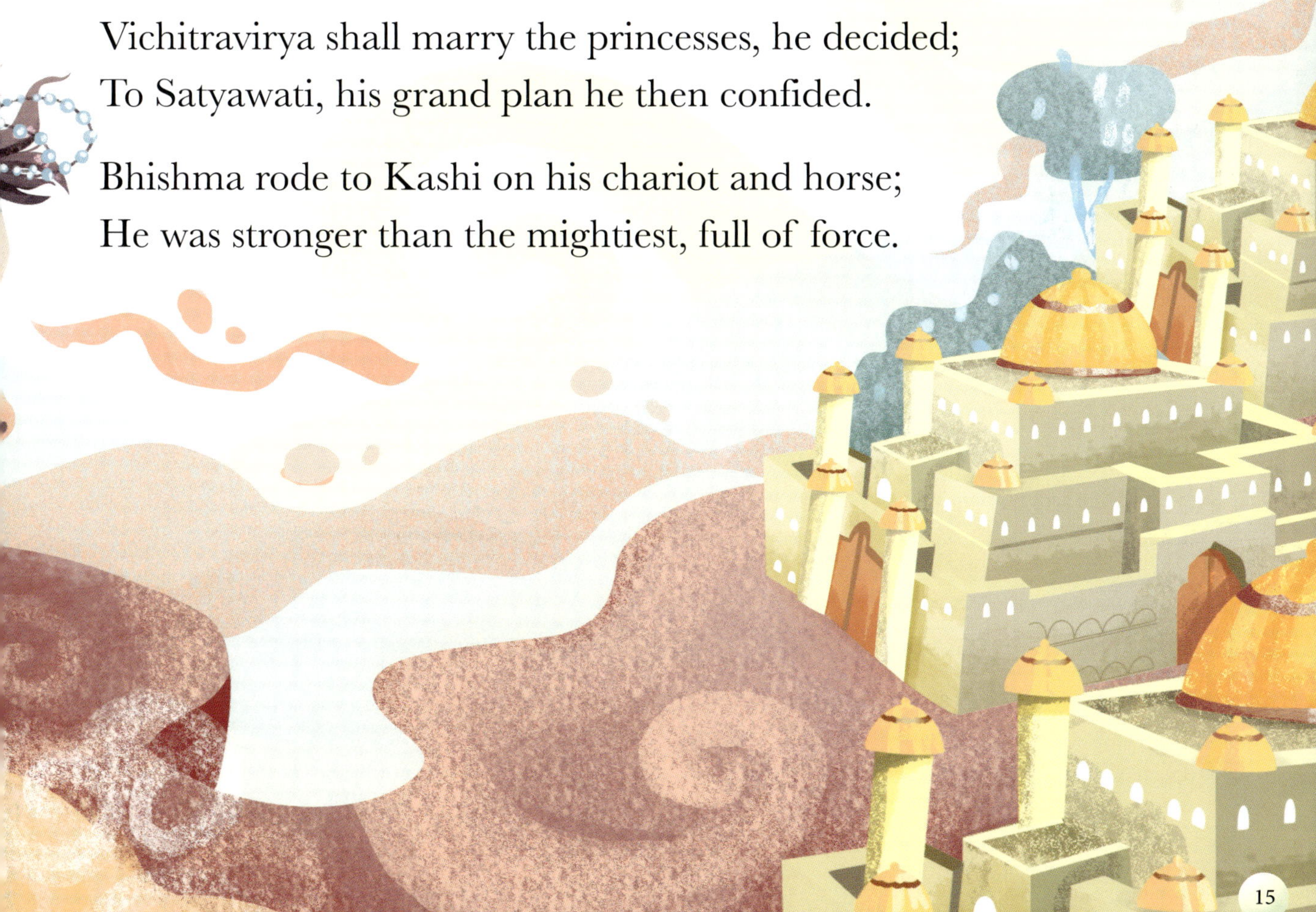

Thinking that Bhishma was breaking his celibacy vow,
The kings mocked and jeered, and ridiculed him, now!

An enraged Bhishma shot an arrow that pierced each crown;
The kings, deeply ashamed, cowered and looked down.

'These princesses shall marry Vichitravirya without a doubt!'
Bhishma loudly announced with a triumphant shout.

Amba, Ambika and Ambalika did not rejoice;
They'd have to marry him, they didn't have a choice.

Amba, who wanted to marry King Shalva, was dejected and sad;
While Ambika and Ambalika were neither angry nor glad.

Vichitravirya, the princesses were to wed;
On Bhishma's chariot, off to Hastinapur they sped.

But King Shalva's army blocked their way;
He wanted his love Amba, right away.

Bhishma and Shalva began a fearsome fight;
Both of them fought with all their might!

Before long, it was Bhishma who easily won;
King Shalva thought his life was over and done.

Bhishma being large-hearted, didn't kill the king;
He told Shalva to go back and forget everything.

When they reached Hastinapur, to Satyawati, Amba said,
'I will not marry Vichitravirya, I would rather be dead.'

Amba told Satyawati about Shalva, and confessed her love;
Then with folded hands, she prayed to the heavens above.

Satyawati asked Bhishma to atone for his deed;
To unite the two lovers would be fair indeed.

Now, when Amba went to Shalva, he only said,
'I can't accept you, you belong to Vichitravirya instead!'

To Hastinapur, when a disheartened Amba returned,
Everyone in the kingdom was gravely concerned.

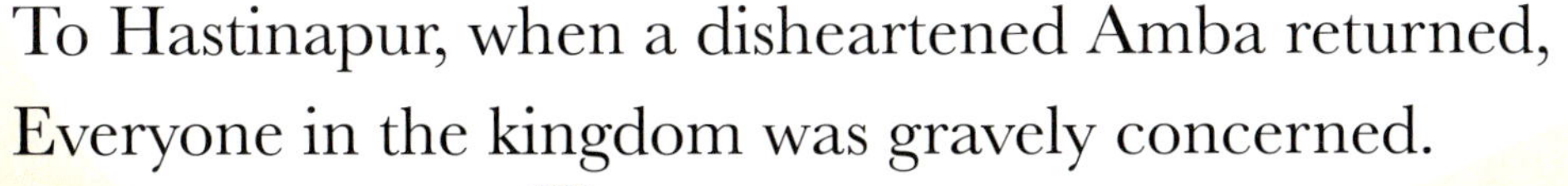

Vichitravirya too, refused Amba's hand;
'She loves Shalva,' he said to clear his stand.

Then, hurt and betrayed, Amba to Bhishma exclaimed,
With a face full of anger, and her eyes inflamed!

'You've ruined me, Bhishma, now marry me!'
But Bhishma had a vow to keep, so how could he?

Trembling with anger, Amba said,
'I'll do anything just to see you dead!

For this, I'll move both heaven and Earth,
Be it in this, or in the coming birth!

But in the end, you, Bhishma, I shall kill!'
She then went away the task to fulfil.

As they were struggling with this affair,
Vichitravirya died without an heir.

No one now knew what to do;
The worry in their hearts just grew, and grew!

One day to the palace, Sage Veda Vyasa came;
The queens can have sons, this was his claim.

As Queen Ambika went into his room,
She was nervous, one can safely assume.

Veda Vyasa looked scary, with his frightful stare;
His repulsive face, she just couldn't bear.

Scared and distressed, she covered her eyes;
Its grave consequences she didn't realise.

Her son Dhritarashtra was born blind at birth;
How would he rule the greatest kingdom on Earth?

With Dhritarashtra, Satyawati was not satisfied;
She thought it was now time that Ambalika tried.

Of Veda Vyasa, Ambalika too was very afraid;
She stared at his face, horrified and dismayed!

At its very sight, she cowered with fear;
And from her eyes fell a single tear.

She gave birth to Pandu who was weak and unwell;
Who would be a better king, was now hard to tell.

Bhishma wanted the two queens to have another try;
But Ambika, Ambalika, both refused, saying they'd rather die!

They secretly sent a maid in their place
Who wasn't afraid to look at Veda Vyasa's face.

The maid's son, Vidura, was healthy and wise;
All future kings he would faithfully advise.

Dhritarashtra, Pandu and Vidura grew under Bhishma's care;
Soon it was time for a decision, just and fair.

The question arose of choosing a king;
Pandu and Dhritarashtra were both in the reckoning.

Dhritarashtra being the oldest, was whom Bhishma chose;
'But that's against Dharma,' said Vidura, and arose.

He said, 'Dhritarashtra is blind, make Pandu the king.'
Much anguish to Bhishma these words did bring.

Finally, Dhritarashtra himself decided to step down;
He spoke seriously, calmly, and without a frown.

'I cannot rule effectively, as I am blind;
Don't make me king just to be kind.

I willingly give the throne to Pandu, my brother;
He will surely make Hastinapur blossom and prosper.'

Pandu, speechless and grateful, was now to be crowned;
Bhishma was glad that a ruler had been found.

Amidst pomp and ceremony, Pandu was sworn-in;
For Hastinapur, it was time for a new era to begin.

Dhritarashtra Becomes King of Hastinapur

It was time for Dhritarashtra's marriage to be decided;
On King Subala's daughter, Bhishma's hopes resided.

He asked Subala for his daughter Gandhari's hand;
She wouldn't be queen, but her life would be grand.

Shakuni, Gandhari's brother was rightly outraged;
'Why Dhritarashtra, and not Pandu?' he loudly raged.

'Doesn't my sister deserve to be queen?
It's the most unfair proposal ever heard or seen!'

Then Gandhari entered, strong and proud!
She looked around, then said aloud:

'I will marry Dhritarashtra although he is blind;
Forever shall I be in his heart, soul and mind.

Then, a cloth upon her eyes she tied,
Which wouldn't be removed till the day she died.

While Bhishma did nothing else, but stare,
Shakuni lamented in great despair.

He warned her that it was a grave mistake,
And said, 'You have put your future at stake!'

But Gandhari and Dhritarashtra still did wed,
While vengeance burned in Shakuni's head.

Now it was time to find King Pandu a wife;
Bhishma wanted his nephew to have a perfect life.

Invites were sent for King Surasena's daughter, Kunti's hand,
To Hastinapur, and all other kingdoms of the land.

Bhishma decided that to Pandu, Kunti must be wed;
It was now time for Pandu to start looking ahead!

Pandu went to King Surasena with a show of strength;
He was determined to return with a wife at length.

And sure enough, when it was Kunti's turn to choose,
She chose Pandu, who had known he'd never lose.

On her wedding day, there were tears on her face;
An old memory stirred, and, in her mind did surface.

Many years ago, Sage Durvasa had come to her palace;
He was tired and looking for a resting place.

Kunti's hospitality pleased him, and soon
The sage granted her a special boon.

A mantra to summon any god or goddess,
To come to Earth and Kunti to bless.

This boon Kunti soon forgot,
For a fulfilling life she had got.

Once, just to see what it was all about,
To the Sun God she ardently called out.

Lo and Behold! the Sun God appeared;
She wanted nothing from him whom she feared.

The Sun God blessed her with a son;
The boon for Kunti was a shocking one.

A son out of marriage was a matter of shame;
Even though she loved him, this son she couldn't claim.

She placed him in a basket which floated down the river;
She sobbed, and wailed, and cried, for she couldn't be his caregiver.

All this, while being wed, Kunti thought;
And to stop her tears, she bravely fought.

Then, determined to be a good wife to Pandu,
She married him without any further ado.

Hastinapur now had a king and a queen;
A better king than Pandu no one could've been.

Hastinapur's borders were huge, with seemingly no end;
Pandu defeated anyone who refused to be his friend.

One day, from a war while he was coming back,
He saw King Madra's army poised for attack.

He commanded his soldiers to be prepared!
But, getting off his chariot, Madra declared:

'For a king, war is an unpleasant task;
So your benign friendship I have come to ask.'

To this proposal, Pandu readily agreed;
They vowed to be friends in thought, word and deed.

Madra gifted Pandu his beloved sister,
Madri, whose beauty enchanted all those who saw her.

Though Madra's intent was obviously well-meant,
Now Pandu found himself in a predicament!

On the one hand, would Madri, Kunti accept?
On the other, a gift turned down meant disrespect.

They rode back to their kingdom, both Madri and he;
The crowd cheered on seeing the lovely Madri!

When introduced to Kunti, Madri touched her feet;
Kunti welcomed and placed her on her rightful seat.

Pandu, as everyone knew, was a great king,
Who diligently took care of everything.

Vidura said,'Pandu, your duties you've never shirked;
You need to rest, how hard you've worked!'

Pandu, Kunti and Madri then went to rest,
Outside the kingdom, to a lovely forest.

One day, while hunting, Pandu shot a deer;
But it wasn't a deer, but a holy seer!

The seer and his wife were hurt and in pain;
King Pandu repented, but in vain!

The dying seer then cursed King Pandu,
Which was the worst thing he could ever do.

He cursed, 'Pandu, if ever again you go near your wife,
It shall cause great pain and end your life!'

Kunti and Madri were shocked and sad;
Now they couldn't have children, which was very bad.

Pandu desperately cried, again and again,
'In the forest forever, I shall remain.'

Dhritarashtra gladly became caretaker of the crown.
He was the one who ultimately brought Hastinapur down.

Krishna's Childhood Leelas

Let us leave Hastinapur, and to Mathura we shall proceed,
Where King Kansa committed every possible evil deed.

He made Kunti's brother, Vasudeva, marry Devaki, his sister dear;
But on their marriage day, he was filled with fear.

For the sky split open, and a celestial voice said,
'Evil Kansa! Devaki's eighth son will strike you dead!'

A worried Kansa put the couple in jail;
He killed Devaki's firstborn, ignoring her wail.

When Devaki gave birth to her second son,
Once again the evil deed was done.

Her third, fourth, fifth and sixth sons died in the same way;
She was devastated, but to Kansa what could she say?

With the birth of the seventh child, Devaki became strong-willed;
She lied that he was stillborn, to save him from being killed.

He'd been given to Rohini, Vasudeva's other wife;
They prayed that this son of theirs would lead a happy life.

Finally, when the birth of her eighth son took place,
A bright light was seen emitting from the child's face.

The guards fell unconscious; Earth became still;
The prison doors opened, perhaps by God's will.

Vasudeva left for Nandagaon, carrying his son amidst a storm;
Sheshnag protected them; he'd recognised Vishnu in the baby's form.

Vasudeva exchanged this son for his friend Nanda's daughter,
Whom the next day, evil King Kansa tried to slaughter.

Kansa said, 'You have a daughter and no eighth son;
With her death, the God's prophecy I have undone.'

Nanda's wife Yashoda was full of joy,
When she saw the angelic infant boy.

Baby Krishna's pranks grew more and more,
Which the gopis of the village would so adore!

He'd steal their butter and tease them lots;
The 'Makhan Chor' would break their earthen pots.

His older brother Balarama too would join in the fun;
No one knew that he was Devaki's seventh son.

Krishna loved music and used to play the flute;
The village gopis loved him for he was very cute.

He played and danced with all, but had only one true love;
She was his real soulmate, recognised by the gods above.

The soulmate's name was Radha, and he played the flute for her;
Though they never wed, inseparable they always were.

One day, the village elders gathered and despaired;
There was a huge snake in the lake, they all were rather scared.

This multi-hooded Kalia, had poisoned their water source;
Nobody dared to face it, nor kill it with mighty force.

The children knew all this, but they didn't care at all;
They happily kept playing near the lake with their ball.

Krishna's friend Sudama had made the ball on his own;
He was fond and very proud of it, this fact was well-known.

Krishna threw the ball and it fell into the lake;
And for poor Sudama, it was too much to take!

He cried, 'Krishna, since you threw it, you go and fetch it back!'
Krishna agreed, even though the water was muddy and black.

He climbed a tree and then, jumped into the lake;
He soon came across that huge monster snake!

He pushed, and pulled, and fought with him;
Krishna kept smiling, the mood was never grim.

Eventually Kalia Naag, the wicked giant snake,
Bowed down, as more pain he could not take.

From the water Krishna arose, dancing on Kalia's head;
Everybody cheered and clapped, they'd thought Krishna was dead!

Then Krishna in his glory, danced his very special dance;
To see a sight so beautiful, one rarely gets a chance.

They treated him with great respect and followed his advice,
For now they knew their Kanha was extraordinary and wise.

Once, as people prayed to Indra, the Hindu god of rain,
Krishna felt it wasn't right, and then said in disdain:

'Why must you only to Indra pray?
Now just pay heed to what I say!

Worship the milk-giving holy cow;
To the Govardhan mountain, pray and bow.

Worship each and every Nature's boon;
The rivers and trees, the sun and the moon.'

Indra showed his anger with thunder and lightning;
He created storms in Nandagaon which were very frightening.

Krishna, on his little finger, lifted the Govardhan;
'Seek shelter in its shade,' he said to everyone.

Indra saw God in Krishna, and asked for forgiveness.
After that, with good weather, Nandagaon he did bless.

Kansa's men saw this, and soon this news was spread;
Kansa now remembered the celestial warning with dread.

He thought, *I had killed my enemy, and the prophecy was undone,*
Then why is it I fear that Krishna is Devaki's eighth son?

He sent a messenger to invite Krishna to come
From Nandagaon, to Mathura, which was Kansa's kingdom.

Yashoda and Radha didn't want Krishna to go;
They were afraid of Kansa, he was a cruel foe.

But Krishna with Balarama went to Mathura and looked around;
They soon saw a structure which was securely bound.

In it was kept Lord Shiva's magical bow!
Krishna couldn't resist; his strength he wanted to show.

When the guards saw Krishna, they started to laugh;
For compared to the bow, in size, Krishna was only half!

But then, Krishna lifted and broke the magical bow!
How the young boy did it, the guards didn't know.

When King Kansa heard, he was very surprised;
How strong Krishna truly was, just then he realised.

Krishna was taken to an arena with no weapon at all;
Before him were five wrestlers, very strong and tall.

The fight began, and of course, Krishna won;
He wasn't even serious, he was just having fun.

Alarmed and enraged, Kansa now entered the fight;
Krishna killed him too, he did what was true and right.

The people of Mathura then joyfully cheered.
Krishna had killed the one they so feared.

Krishna and Balarama then set their parents free;
They had fulfilled a part of their destiny.

On seeing Krishna, Devaki smiled and hugged her son;
The wait was over, and good over evil had finally won.

Krishna's grandfather Ugrasena was then appointed king;
He was wise and would always do the right thing.

Krishna and Balarama then went to Sandipani Ashram school;
Some day, they would play an important part in Hastinapur's rule.

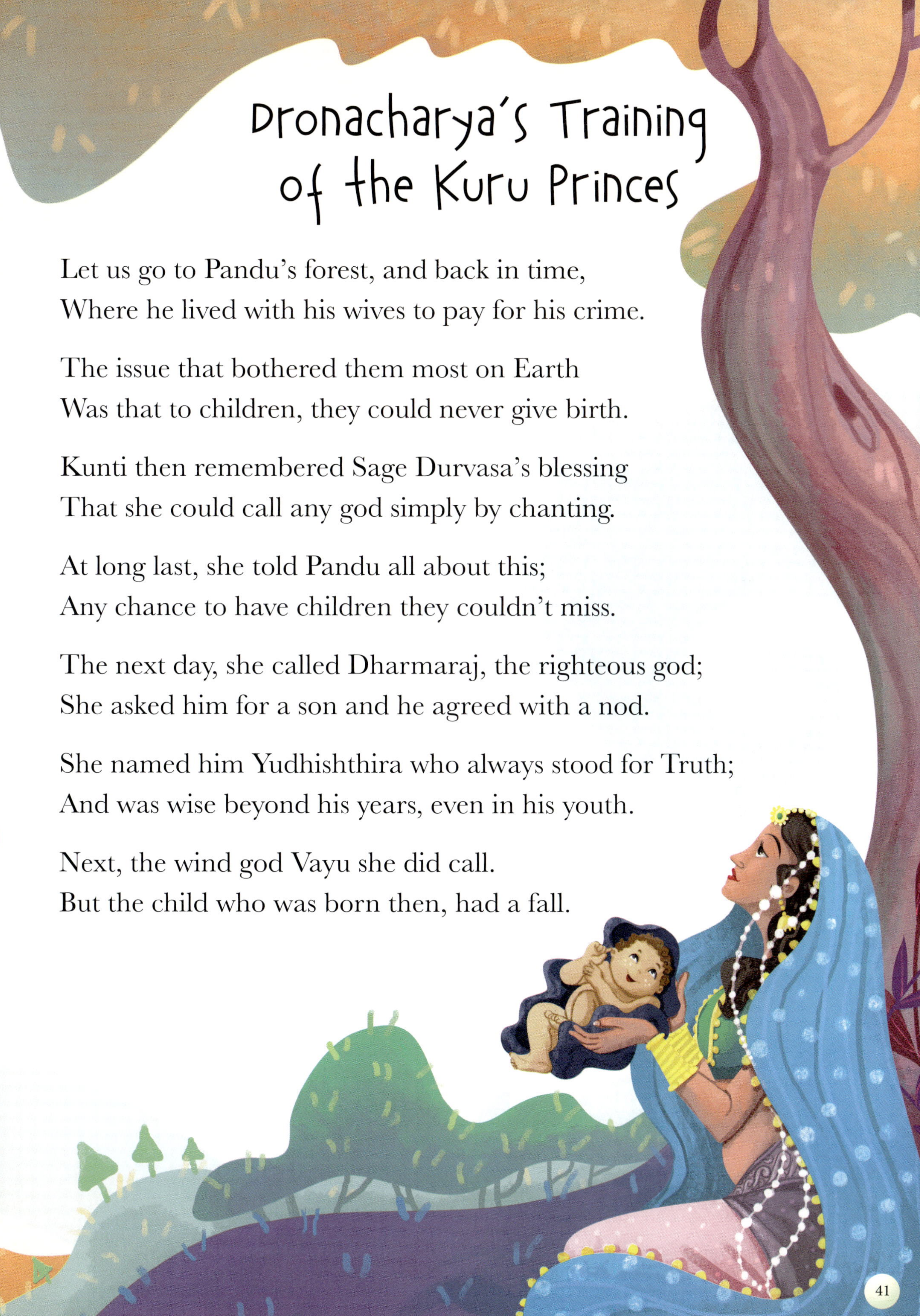

Dronacharya's Training of the Kuru Princes

Let us go to Pandu's forest, and back in time,
Where he lived with his wives to pay for his crime.

The issue that bothered them most on Earth
Was that to children, they could never give birth.

Kunti then remembered Sage Durvasa's blessing
That she could call any god simply by chanting.

At long last, she told Pandu all about this;
Any chance to have children they couldn't miss.

The next day, she called Dharmaraj, the righteous god;
She asked him for a son and he agreed with a nod.

She named him Yudhishthira who always stood for Truth;
And was wise beyond his years, even in his youth.

Next, the wind god Vayu she did call.
But the child who was born then, had a fall.

He didn't hurt himself, but broke a large stone!
Kunti named him Bhima for his mighty strength alone.

Which God to call next? she wondered, to have another son.
Meanwhile, her nephew Krishna had been born in a Mathura prison.

Finally, Lord Indra she decided to summon,
From whom she got Arjuna, her youngest son.

Now Madri too, wanted to mother an heir;
So with her too, the mantra, Kunti did share.

Madri chanted the mantra, a god to summon;
She called the Ashwin twins, the sons of the Sun.

They gave her the twins, Nakula and Sahadeva;
They would grow up to be just and brave.

Some years later, as Pandu was going to meditate,
He fell victim at the hands of cruel fate.

Attracted by Madri's irresistible charms,
He went to embrace her in his arms.

He forgot the curse and time stood still;
The temptation took over his rather weak will.

Suddenly, his body went limp, and soon he died.
Madri was devastated! She cried, and cried.

On Pandu's funeral, Madri jumped into the flame,
For she felt and believed that she was to blame.

Kunti and the Pandavas then returned to the palace,
Distressed, and with sadness written on each face.

When Dhritarashtra heard of Pandu's untimely death,
He began to perceive the Pandavas as a threat.

For, despite his daughter Dushala and a hundred sons,
Kunti's son Yudhishthira was the eldest of the young ones.

Dhritarashtra wanted Duryodhana, his eldest son, to wear the crown;
While evil Shakuni just waited to bring the Pandavas down.

Dhritarashtra, with a maid, also had a son named Yuyutsu,
Who was very wise and supported anyone who was true.

Meanwhile, Adhiratha, Dhritarashtra's charioteer decided to resign;
'I need time to take care of the adopted son of mine!'

Said Adhiratha, who lived near the river Ganga with his wife;
They had been unhappy as they were living a childless life.

But then, one day they had heard a baby cry;
In a floating basket, he had been left to die.

He was wearing a golden armour, and earrings that shone!
They named him Karna and raised him as their own.

Adhiratha found another charioteer, Sanjay, who was loyal too,
And would wisely serve Dhritarashtra through and through.

Meanwhile, the Kauravas and Pandavas couldn't enhance their skill,
As the family guru Kripacharya had some other tasks to fulfil.

One day, Dronacharya, who was Kripacharya's brother-in-law,
Was passing through Hastinapur, and the Kuru princes he saw.

Bhishma requested him to train the princes, and make them great,
So that they could be ready to meet the challenges of their fate.

Their studies began, and Yudhishthira excelled in the spear,
While Nakula and Sahadeva fought with swords, without fear!

Bhima and Duryodhana mastered fighting with the mace,
And they often fought each other, face to face.

Shakuni hated the Pandavas from the depths of his soul!
To destroy them all was his ultimate goal.

So he planned to kill the five Pandavas, one by one;
He believed the throne belonged only to Gandhari's eldest son.

He made Duryodhana feed Bhima porridge laced with poison,
For Shakuni wanted to kill Pandu's strongest son.

As Bhima lay down, and appeared to have died,
Duryodhana and Dushasana in a sack had him tied.

They quickly went and threw him into a lake,
But the Kaurava brothers had made a big mistake.

A group of Nagas found him, who lived near by;
One sucked off the poison; and Bhima did not die!

Before their mighty Naga king, Bhima was then produced;
Himself as Kunti's son, he proudly introduced.

'I am Kuntibhoja,' and, placing his hand on Bhima's strong head,
'I'm Kunti's adoptive father,' the Naga king then said.

He gave Bhima a potion, and his lost strength soon revived;
Kunti's joy knew no bounds, her beloved son had survived.

The Pandavas now understood their cousins' ill-intent,
That any action from their side could never be well-meant.

Meanwhile, Arjuna's skill at archery, was famed across the land;
His concentration was great, he had a very steady hand.

Dronacharya well knew that Arjuna was the very best;
But to prove this before others, he gave them all a test.

They were to shoot the eye of a fake bird, hung high upon a tree;
Then he asked them one by one, what each of them could see.

All, except Arjuna, saw the bird, the tree, the sky;
The dissatisfied Dronacharya now asked Arjuna to give it a try.

Arjuna said, 'I can only see that bird's eye.'
Dronacharya was happy and then he asked him, 'Why?'

Arjuna said his goal was all that mattered to him;
Everything else around him, appeared as very dim.

Dronacharya was pleased; he knew the boy was right;
Arjuna was the greatest archer, who would win any fight.

But there was another archer who matched Arjuna's skill;
His name was Eklavya and he had twice the will.

Dronacharya had refused to teach this boy, born in a lower caste;
For, together with the royal princes, he would only be seen last.

When Dronacharya asked who taught him,
His expression changed from happy to grim!

'Sir, you have been my inspiration, and my guiding light;
This mud statue of yours has never left my sight.

Your idol taught me everything,' thus the boy did claim;
Dronacharya then asked him a gurudakshina for the same.

'I demand your right thumb,' said Dronacharya to the lad,
Eklavya's perfection in archery, for Arjuna, would be bad.

Eklavya in a flash, with his sword cut off his thumb;
As if it didn't pain him, as if his hand was numb.

Dronacharya thus protected Arjuna once, but could not do it forever;
Another boy was about to appear, who would be the best archer ever.

The Kuru princes grew older, stronger, and had no fear;
But who would rule Hastinapur, it was still not clear.

Rangabhoomi

When the princes had learnt their skills, a rangabhoomi was decided,
Where they would showcase their talents, while the king presided.

All the villagers came to watch, when the day of the rangabhoomi arrived;
They sat eagerly in the stadium, to see how the young princes had thrived.

Bhishma sat beside Dhritarashtra, who was sitting on the throne;
Kunti and Gandhari both sat in a separate booth of their own.

Dronacharya and Kripacharya were watching the crowd swell;
Ashwatthama, Dronacharya's son, was sitting there as well.

First, prince Yudhishthira entered, and bowed before the king;
Dhritarashtra was happy, and fondly gave him his blessing.

Duryodhana, Bhima, Dushasana, Arjuna, Nakula, Sahadeva,
Then entered the grand stadium, looking very strong and brave.

In the spear, amongst all the princes, Yudhishthira had won;
Until he and Arjuna faced each other one on one.

It was a very close and intense fight,
But Yudhishthira won with his skill and might.

Next, Ashwatthama announced it was time to showcase
Bhima and Duryodhana, who were fighting with the mace.

The duel prolonged, as they fought and fought.
About defeat, neither of them gave a single thought!

The fight would never end, Dronacharya did realise;
Ashwatthama had to stop them, as per his father's advice.

Now Arjuna was to showcase his talent with the bow;
From the middle of the stadium, he shot an arrow.

Around himself he created a big wall of fire!
He then used an arrow to raise himself higher.

Arjuna made it rain as his arrow shot through the sky;
He also made a rainbow, causing a collective, happy sigh.

Arjuna then made a wall of sticks;
He did many more feats and tricks.

He showcased his tremendous skill;
It seemed he could do anything as per his will.

Dronacharya then stood up and announced,
'Arjuna is the best archer in the world,' he pronounced.

Just then, Adhiratha's adopted son Karna came,
And the title of the best archer he did claim.

Her son, by his armour and earrings, Kunti did recognise;
She had thought him dead all along, she couldn't believe her eyes!

She longed to claim him as her dearest first-born son,
But she would then be ruined, after all that she had done.

'Who are you?' Dronacharya asked as he took him aside;
'I am Karna, Sage Parashurama's disciple,' Karna then replied.

Sage Parashurama was the best teacher on Earth;
He had taught Bhishma and Dronacharya, proving his worth.

'I shall fight and defeat Arjuna,' said Karna sounding grand;
'I will prove that I am the best archer in all the land.'

Karna then shot a magical arrow, using his bow;
Showering water and fire, he created a spectacular show!

Dronacharya stopped Karna, and said in a sharp tone:
'You can't participate if you didn't descend from a throne!'

Karna kept quiet, he didn't reveal his identity to anyone!
How could he tell the world that he was just a charioteer's son?

Duryodhana, recognising Karna's strength, made him his friend;
He wanted to humiliate the Pandavas and have an ally till the end.

So, appointing Karna as ruler of Anga, a princely state,
Duryodhana said that Karna was now eligible to participate.

Thanking Duryodhana for making him a part of royalty,
Karna said, 'Duryodhana, for this, you will have my undying loyalty.'

When Adhiratha heard of his son becoming a king,
He rushed to the stadium, he wanted to know everything.

When Bhima and Arjuna learnt that Karna was the son of a charioteer,
They ridiculed and mocked him, and said with a jeer,

'Arjuna shan't compete with a low caste born!'
These words pricked Karna's pride like a thorn.

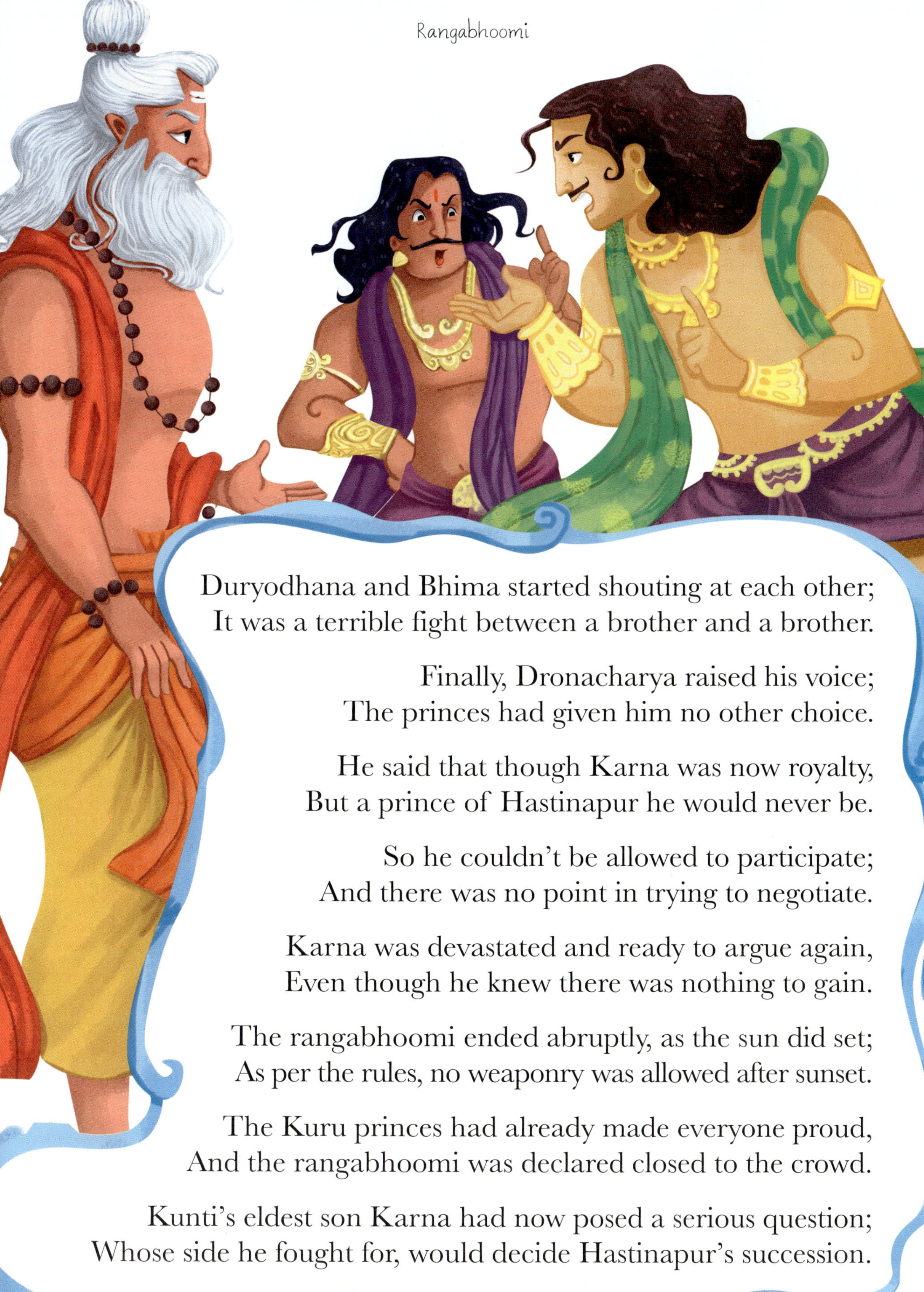

Duryodhana and Bhima started shouting at each other;
It was a terrible fight between a brother and a brother.

Finally, Dronacharya raised his voice;
The princes had given him no other choice.

He said that though Karna was now royalty,
But a prince of Hastinapur he would never be.

So he couldn't be allowed to participate;
And there was no point in trying to negotiate.

Karna was devastated and ready to argue again,
Even though he knew there was nothing to gain.

The rangabhoomi ended abruptly, as the sun did set;
As per the rules, no weaponry was allowed after sunset.

The Kuru princes had already made everyone proud,
And the rangabhoomi was declared closed to the crowd.

Kunti's eldest son Karna had now posed a serious question;
Whose side he fought for, would decide Hastinapur's succession.

Gurudakshina

The Kuru princes had grown into fine young men.
They were ready to move on in life, again.

It was time to pay their gurudakshina, an offering to their guru;
What Dronacharya was about to ask, they didn't have any clue.

Dronacharya then told them, their training was complete,
And if they worked together, they could perform any feat.

As gurudakshina, arrogant Duryodhana offered a lot of gold;
Dronacharya said, 'No! Of my gurudakshina, you'll soon be told.'

But before I tell you what Dronacharya wanted, a story I will narrate;
To understand the present, you must know the events before this date.

When Dronacharya was young, his father was Prince Drupada's Guru;
They grew fond of one another, their friendship was firm and true.

When Drupada's training was complete, they were sad to go apart;
But before they separated, they had a touching heart-to-heart.

Drupada said, 'Whatever is mine, I will share with you,
And whatever is yours, will be half mine too!'

Now, years later, when their son Ashwatthama was born,
Dronacharya and his wife Kripi's hearts were torn.

Kripi said, 'We have no milk to feed our son,
Without which he won't be able to walk or run!'

Dronacharya remembered Drupada's promise made years before,
So he went to Drupada's palace and knocked at his door.

When Drupada heard Dronacharya, he laughed and said,
'Old promises like that are now done and dead!

I am a king, while you are a poor teacher, though wise,
The past is over for both you and me, don't you realise?

Ask me for anything, as you are a man we all respect,
But to be treated as my equal, you please do not expect.'

Dronacharya left from there, with a heart heavy as lead;
The cruel words of Drupada kept churning in his head.

Now we come back to the present, Dronacharya knew the time was right;
So he asked the Kaurava princes, to avenge for that slight.

Duryodhana, with his brothers, went with the Hastinapur army.
He was rather vain and thought, *Who can ever harm me?*

The Pandavas were offended that the Kauravas had been sent;
So they asked Dronacharya, what all this possibly meant.

Dronacharya said, 'Duryodhana still has a lesson left to learn;
Arrogance he has to forget and respect he has to earn!'

Duryodhana tried, but failed, and disheartened he came back;
To Dronacharya he described King Drupada's army's attack.

He apologised for failing to fulfil his guru's task;
'What else can I do for you?' he meekly then did ask.

Dronacharya said, 'You tried, and I think that is enough!'
Then the Pandavas were given the task, which was very tough.

The Pandavas went to fight, with no army by their side,
For Dronacharya had asked them alone, and no one from outside.

The Pandavas were just five but fought as one;
Their skills were unbeatable by anyone.

They succeeded in defeating Drupada's army;
And then took Drupada into their custody.

When Dronacharya saw they had returned with success,
He was delighted, and told Drupada who was in deep stress:

'You have been defeated by my students with whom you fought,
But I shall keep my promise to share, even though you did not.'

Dronacharya took half of Drupada's kingdom, but spared his life;
And took one extra cow to please Kripi, his beloved wife.

When Kripi saw Dronacharya after all that while,
All she could manage was a weak smile.

Meanwhile, Drupada was disturbed and wanted revenge;
Later on, his pride he would definitely try to avenge.

Now, on the other side, in Sage Sandipani's school,
Krishna had grown up and was ready to rule.

For Krishna and Balarama, it was time to leave;
Blessings from Sage Sandipani and his wife they did receive.

They were their foster parents and didn't want them to go;
What gurudakshina to give them, Balarama did not know.

But Krishna knew that demons had kidnapped their dearest son;
Nothing to them would matter more than having him return.

So Krishna and Balarama went out, searching far and wide;
They soon returned happily, with the boy by their side.

The delighted parents saw their son after many years;
Krishna and Balarama left the school, amidst their happy tears.

On their way to Mathura, to meet Krishna and Balarama,
Came the great teacher and warrior, Sage Parashurama!

He gave Krishna the Sudarshan Chakra, Lord Vishnu's weapon;
Which could only be used by Krishna since he and Vishnu were one.

Parashurama reminded Krishna, 'You were born to do God's will;
For the greater good of mankind, an important role to fulfil!'

Krishna knew everything and was just playing his part;
For Hastinapur, the days of misery were now about to start.

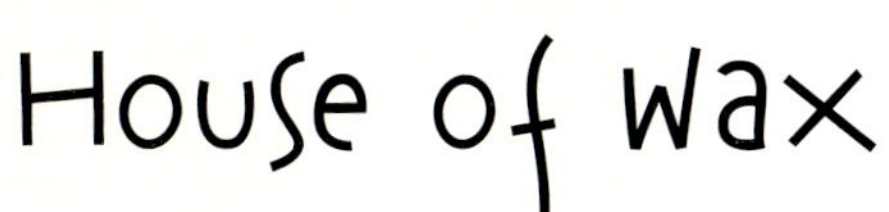

House of Wax

Meanwhile in Hastinapur, a tough decision was near;
For Bhishma, all his grand-nephews were equally dear.

It was time to choose Hastinapur's next king;
For this decision, everyone had been anxiously waiting.

As the elders contemplated who'd be the best one to rule;
Shakuni secretly hatched a plan that was both evil and cruel.

He tried to convince Dhritarashtra of his evil plan,
Which would make his son Duryodhana the ruler of the clan.

Everyone considered that Yudhishthira was the best;
The matter of the crown should now have been put to rest.

Normally the eldest son is crowned as future king;
But in Hastinapur, this wasn't solving anything.

Duryodhana's father Dhritarashtra was currently on the throne;
But Pandu's son Yudhishthira for righteousness was known.

For Dhritarashtra, it was a tough decision to take;
His son Duryodhana, the king he wanted to make.

But when the day of the decision came,
He did not want to take all the blame.

So he said that Yudhishthira would be Hastinapur's heir;
Duryodhana thought his father's decision was most unfair.

He watched the grand coronation with envy in his heart;
To explore the kingdom, then the Pandavas did depart.

I must find a way to destroy them, Shakuni thought,
With Duryodhana and Karna, he discussed his evil plot.

In Varnavrat, the festival of Shiva was drawing near,
Which the king or the crown prince visited every year.

They told the king if Yudhishthira would
Go to Varnavrat instead of him, it would be good.

Shakuni called an architect and asked him to build
A house made of wax, to have the Pandavas killed!

For, a house made of wax could easily burn;
Then, in their favour the situation would turn.

Yudhishthira, his brothers and Kunti decided to go;
It was a conspiracy to kill them, this they didn't know.

When Vidura heard of the Pandavas' journey, he grew suspicious,
For he knew that the Kauravas were wicked and very vicious.

So his trusted spies were then sent to investigate;
But, Oh! Alas! it had already become quite late.

Vidura's spy informed him that a wax house had been made;
Which, for the lives of the Pandavas, made Vidura truly afraid.

On the day the Pandavas left, he finally figured it out;
That this was an evil plan, now he absolutely had no doubt.

He sent a miner with a message that filled the Pandavas with rage!
Yudhishthira calmed them down, being the oldest of them in age.

Vidura's miner built a tunnel which was hidden;
A mention or a talk of it was then forbidden.

The Pandavas and Kunti lit a fire and escaped,
And made it appear that no one had been saved.

When the news finally reached Shakuni's ears,
He was delighted and it took away all his fears.

He thought that the Pandavas and Kunti were dead,
And not a suspicious word had been said.

When Dhritarashtra found out, he loudly cried!
He couldn't believe that all the Pandavas had died.

Dronacharya and Kripacharya too were devastated;
They had never been so helpless and agitated.

But when Bhishma heard, his world turned black!
He couldn't believe it, he wanted time to go back.

He locked himself in his room,
And was full of misery and gloom.

After many days, he opened his door;
His soul was hurting, and his heart was sore.

He went to meet Goddess Ganga, his mother dear,
Who consoled him, 'Bhishma, son, have no fear,

The Pandavas and dear Kunti are alive and well;
Ask Vidura, the full story he'll be able to tell.'

A furious Bhishma called Vidura to explain;
'How could you let me live with all this pain?'

He wanted to know where the Pandavas were;
Vidura couldn't answer as even he wasn't sure.

So Bhishma went off, angry and thundering!
Where were the Pandavas? You too must be wondering.

The Kauravas and Pandavas were now clearly divided;
But Hastinapur's fate was yet to be decided!

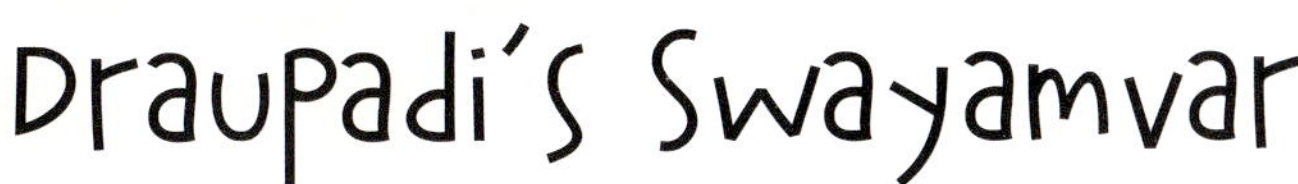

Draupadi's Swayamvar

The Pandavas in a forest were forced to hide;
Their next step they were yet to decide.

Demon Hidimbasura also lived there with his sister;
He would eat people and was very strong and sinister.

His sister Hidimbi was equally strong, but kind and wise;
She fell in love with Bhima, before he could realise.

While Hidimbasura wanted to eat the Pandavas and celebrate,
Hidimbi wanted to save them, she considered Bhima a soulmate.

She used her powers and helped Bhima kill her brother;
A thankful Bhima offered something in return to please her.

Hidimbi then asked Bhima to marry her, and even did plead;
Bhima was surprised, but as he had promised, he agreed.

So Bhima, Kunti and the Pandavas stayed with her for a while;
Then she gave birth to a strong and brave boy with a smile.

Bhima wanted to stay, but Kunti told him it was time to leave;
There were other things that the Pandavas were born to achieve.

The Pandavas cleverly went hiding from place to place,
Ensuring that they did not leave behind their smallest trace.

One day, with some sages they were eating their food;
They were all in a pleasant and relaxed mood.

A sage mentioned an upcoming event in the land;
Suitors had been invited to seek Draupadi's hand.

'Who is this Draupadi?' Arjuna finally did ask.
To tell you fellow readers, it is quite a difficult task.

After Dronacharya humiliated him, Drupada was furious!
He went to Lord Shiva to ask about his fate, as he was curious.

His only son Shikhandi, was born as a weak eunuch;
I do need another son, thought Drupada, cursing his luck.

After many fervent prayers, Lord Shiva granted him a boon,
Which Drupada hoped and prayed would come true very soon.

Shiva granted him a daughter, along with one more son;
For Dronacharya's destruction, this son would be the reason.

While the daughter would be known for her beauty,
She would be born to also fulfil an important duty.

Drupada then performed a yagya, to fulfil his desire;
As a result, a son and a daughter were born out of the fire.

Dhrishtadyumna and Draupadi were kept as their names;
To avenge their father, they emerged fully grown from the flames.

As for Shikhandi's story, a bit you'll have to wait;
For now, we will focus only on Draupadi and her fate.

Let's go back to the Pandavas, who were by then so awestruck
On hearing of Draupadi's beauty, they wished to try their luck.

The Pandavas dressed as sages, then set out to see,
Which king would go home with Draupadi, as a sign of victory?

At the event, King Drupada had set up a special moving target,
To be viewed through its reflection and almost impossible to get!

There was another condition which everyone should know;
The kings were not allowed to use their own bow and arrow.

King Drupada announced the start, and when the first king came,
He couldn't even lift the bow so he went back feeling lame.

They had to use Lord Shiva's bow, which Drupada had provided;
This task was very difficult, all the kings decided.

They all tried their level best but no one could succeed;
One by one, they failed; their defeat they had to concede.

Finally, it was the King of Anga, Karna's turn;
If he succeeded, respect he would earn!

Karna, Sage Parashurama's disciple, towered above them all;
Amongst all other kings and warriors, he clearly stood proud and tall.

Paying his guru respect, he picked up Lord Shiva's bow;
Karna, with his archery skills, was now ready for the show!

But before Karna could go ahead and take the final aim,
Draupadi said, 'He's a charioteer's son,' putting him to shame.

She didn't want to marry a mere charioteer's son;
Karna, fuming with rage, sat down, feeling undone!

With no king left, Drupada asked the sages to give it a try;
Arjuna looked at Yudhishthira, who nodded in reply.

Arjuna paid his respects and picked up the bow with ease;
He notched his arrow and went down on his knees.

On his very first try, Arjuna easily hit the target;
This was a moment no one would ever forget!

Then all the kings got up together in a rage!
How could Draupadi possibly marry a sage?

They shouted that Draupadi had to make a choice;
Draupadi during all this, couldn't find her voice.

Arjuna came up to her dressed like a sage;
Draupadi coyly garlanded him, despite all the outrage.

Yudhishthira and the twins then decided to leave;
Bhima would protect Arjuna, they firmly did believe.

Bhima and Duryodhana fought with each other;
Then Arjuna and Karna came in front of one another.

Arjuna shot an arrow and broke Karna's bow;
Duryodhana with the others, then decided to go.

Draupadi had chosen her husband as per Drupada's plan;
She would bring Hastinapur down and ruin the Kuru clan.

Division of Hastinapur

Arjuna and Bhima escorted Draupadi to their forest,
Where their brothers were waiting, getting some rest.

Arjuna suggested, 'Let us tell mother we have brought a lot of food;
When she will see Draupadi, it will put her in a good mood.'

When they entered their little hut, they just plainly said,
'Look mother, what we have brought, food and lots of bread!'

Kunti didn't turn around, but just asked them to share;
The five brothers were stupefied and couldn't look anywhere.

When Kunti turned around, she saw a lovely maid;
Draupadi, the bride, stood there, trembling and afraid.

'Who is this girl?' Kunti asked, showing her surprise;
In a flash, her big mistake she then did realise.

'Why did you refer to her as food?' Kunti said in an angry way;
'Do you all not realise the price you'll have to pay?'

Arjuna replied with remorse in his voice,
'We will have to share her, now we have no choice!

You have given us your instructions, mother,
We now have to share her with one another.'

'I thought you were talking about food,' Kunti shouted;
'Now, what do we do?' she said, while Draupadi pouted.

Just then at the scene, Lord Krishna did arrive;
He greeted his aunt Kunti, and all the brothers five.

Krishna explained that this was Draupadi's written fate;
In her previous birth, her husband wasn't accomplished or great.

Therefore, to Lord Shiva, day and night she would pray,
To give her such a man who was perfect in every way.

She wanted to be wedded to the most righteous man on Earth,
Who was the bravest and the strongest to have ever taken birth.

Bhima was very strong, while Yudhishthira was always right;
But Draupadi wanted something more, she prayed with all her might.

She wanted the most skilled archer of all;
Arjuna alone could have answered that call.

She wanted the most truthful and handsome man there;
Nakula and Sahadeva answered this fair and square.

While all this took place, Dhrishtadyumna on them spied;
His sister was married to the Pandavas, he thought with lots of pride.

He informed his father, who too was very pleased;
This opportunity to befriend the Pandavas, he quickly seized.

He said, 'Please be our honoured guests, for as long as you desire,
Because all your great deeds and virtues, we sincerely do admire.'

When the news reached Hastinapur, Duryodhana was surprised;
That the Pandavas were still alive, he suddenly realised.

Vidura told Dhritarashtra to call the Pandavas back;
Dhritarashtra could not refuse, as such courage he did lack.

After the Pandavas had supposedly died,
Duryodhana as crown prince was naturally implied.

Now the question was, who would rule in the end?
Dhritarashtra asked everyone the best man to recommend.

They discussed for hours, and hours, but no decision came;
Then Bhishma gave a suggestion which was sad, but fair all the same!

He regretfully suggested that Hastinapur should be divided;
After many tears and discussions, this option was decided.

When Duryodhana heard this, he was angry and also sad;
But a cunning solution to this problem, Uncle Shakuni had.

He told Dhritarashtra to give the Pandavas the terrible demons' land,
Known as Khandavprastha, even going there should have been banned.

When the Pandavas came back, all was forgiven;
From Dhritarashtra, the news they were given.

They took their given half without any complaint,
Although Arjuna had to be held with plenty of restraint.

One son each from Draupadi, the Pandava brothers got;
They were happy with their fortune, delighted with their lot.

Reaching Khandavprastha, they were disappointed by what they saw;
Covered with only thorns and weeds, this barren land was raw.

Krishna advised Arjuna to use his arrow and bow;
To Bhima, he gave a shovel, so that the land he could sow.

He asked them to make Khandavprastha green,
And turn it into the most beautiful place ever seen.

They worked hard, and prayed to Indra, the god of rain,
To bless their kingdom with showers, to fill the land with grain.

The Pandavas killed the demons who didn't cooperate;
But some of them survived and helped to build the state.

One demon, Maya, made a palace of illusion;
It was beautiful, but would fill you with confusion.

Finally, the great city of Indraprastha was made;
In honour of Lord Indra, it was rightly named.

Then Yudhishthira was crowned as the rightful king;
The Pandavas now had almost everything.

Although Indraprastha was everything a king could desire;
Hastinapur was by now a weak and divided empire.

Yudhishthira Performs the Rajsuya Yagya

Krishna asked Yudhishthira to do the Rajsuya yagya, a ceremony;
It was performed to show their strength and bring harmony.

For Yudhishthira, to be declared the greatest,
He would first have to go through a difficult test.

A king named Jarasandha was very powerful;
He was a devotee of Lord Shiva, but extremely cruel!

He wanted to capture one hundred kings to sacrifice;
Lord Shiva he wanted to please by paying this price.

Jarasandha would then be undefeatable forever;
And Yudhishthira would never become the ruler.

To prevent this, they would have to kill him;
But in a war, their chances for a win were rather slim.

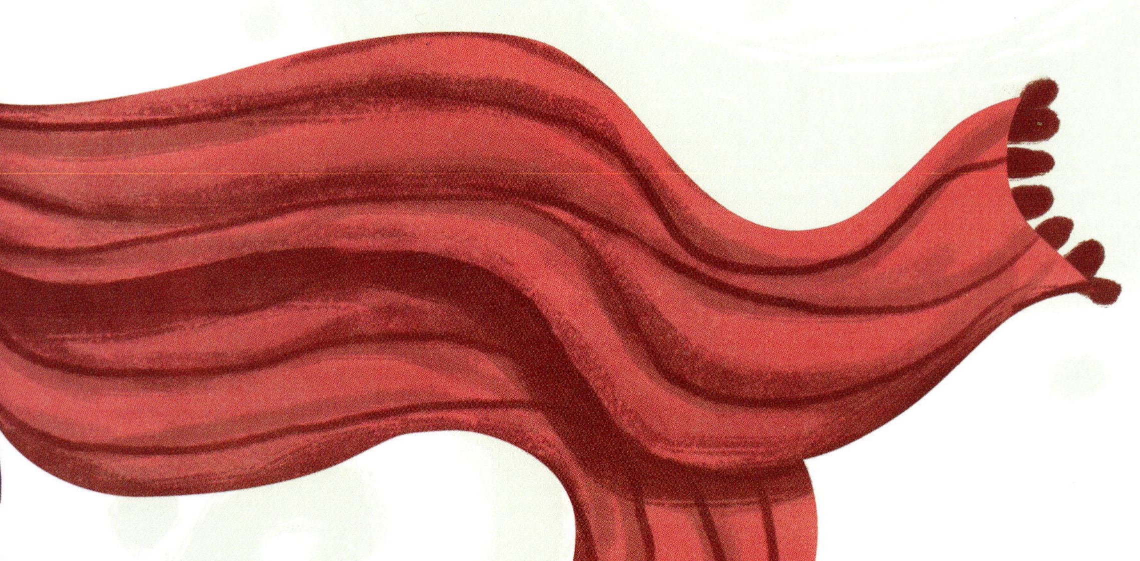

For Jarasandha had a massive army, which was hard to defeat;
Yudhishthira asked Krishna for help in accomplishing this feat.

Krishna told them, 'I will tell you a story.
To defeat him, you must know his history!

Long ago, Jarasandha's father had two wives;
He vowed that as long as he was alive,

He would love both his wives equally.
But he didn't have any sons, unfortunately!

He was worried that soon he would be old in age,
So he went to pray and be blessed by a sage.

The sage gave him a mango for one wife,
Which would help her give birth to a new life.

Jarasandha's father now faced a problem.
To give that mango to which of them?

He just couldn't bear to break his vow;
He was confused as to what he should do now.

He broke the mango and gave half to each;
He couldn't wait to have a son to teach.

A few months later, each wife bore a child;
But they were half a baby each, their looks were wild.

Both the queens, scared, threw away their half;
A monster named Jara found them and began to laugh.

She put the halves together and the baby became whole;
This child named Jarasandha now had a proper soul.'

Krishna ended the story and the Pandavas were still;
They realised that Jarasandha would be difficult to kill!

'You can't defeat him in battle,' Krishna then said,
'Only in a duel, you can try to strike him dead.'

Disguised as Brahmanas, Arjuna, Bhima and Krishna would go;
Jarasandha would accept the duel, their identity he wouldn't know.

The plan worked, and Jarasandha agreed to fight Bhima;
For Arjuna and Krishna looked weak and were no match, it did seem.

Jarasandha and Bhima began wrestling with each other;
In terms of strength, they were equal to one another.

Soon, Jarasandha realised Bhima was not a normal Brahmana;
But with power and confidence, he could easily be won.

Bhima wrestled Jarasandha and broke him into half;
Arjuna was happy and started celebrating on his behalf.

But Jarasandha's two halves rejoined, and he started to fight;
Bhima broke him again and threw him out of sight.

Jarasandha's halves re-joined again, and Bhima realised his mistake;
For the last time, Jarasandha into two halves he did break.

But this time, he threw the left half to the right,
And threw the right half to the left, with all his might!

Arjuna and Krishna cheered as Jarasandha died;
This astonishing news soon spread far and wide.

Bhima, Krishna and Arjuna freed the captured kings,
And returned to Indraprastha to give Yudhishthira the glad tidings.

Yudhishthira planned the Rajsuya Yagya, his sovereignty to claim;
With Krishna's support, the other kings he wanted to tame.

Some kings were not happy, and opposed Yudhishthira's plan;
This included the Trigarta kingdom which the Trigarta brothers ran.

These princes Arjuna soon defeated and did humiliate;
They vowed to take revenge, and for the right time decided to wait.

When Duryodhana heard about the Yagya, his envy grew;
Yudhishthira would be the greatest king anyone ever knew.

Duryodhana, Shakuni and Karna started to plot;
They were not happy with what the Pandavas had got.

When they came to Indraprastha, they were surprised;
How beautiful the kingdom was, they had not realised.

Duryodhana went inside the palace of illusion,
Which was far beyond his wildest imagination.

Duryodhana saw a pool which was actually a wall!
Then he saw a carpet which was a pond after all!

He took a step on it, and fell headfirst, in the water;
Draupadi saw him and could not control her laughter.

She tauntingly reminded him that he was a blind man's son;
Duryodhana left the palace without waiting for the Yagya to be done.

The Yagya took place and did succeed;
As king of kings, Yudhishthira would now lead.

Duryodhana returned to Hastinapur burning with envy,
And thought, *The Pandavas are my sworn enemy!*

Yudhishthira was declared the most powerful of them all;
Duryodhana's jealousy would cause Hastinapur's downfall.

The Dice Game

Shakuni wanted to invite the Pandavas for a game of dice;
He knew that gambling was Yudhishthira's one and only vice.

He convinced Dhritarashtra that it was a gesture of goodwill;
And Duryodhana's desire for revenge this game would fulfil.

The message was delivered to the Pandavas who agreed;
For Yudhishthira thought that it will improve relations indeed.

The Pandavas, along with Draupadi, went for the dice match;
They were unaware of the plan that Shakuni did hatch.

They were getting ready to play when Duryodhana said,
'My uncle Shakuni will play for me instead!'

Shakuni was almost invincible in the game of dice;
The Pandavas fell into the trap, despite being wise.

The game began with Yudhishthira betting small things;
Gold coins, silver necklaces, bracelets and rings.

Then he put all his servants and ministers at stake,
Which Shakuni, with a roll of dice was able to take.

He bet all his money and riches as well;
What was going to happen now, nobody could tell.

The next thing at stake was Indraprastha, his state;
Now Yudhishthira had almost nothing else left on his plate.

He did something despicable and bad!
He did something no man ever had!

He put his brothers at stake, and lost them one by one;
This was an evil game, it was not a game for fun.

Yudhishthira, disheartened, wanted to end the game;
He no longer had anything left to his name.

Duryodhana, wanting revenge, urged him to bet his wife;
For Draupadi had insulted him and caused this strife.

Yudhishthira, with no other choice left to him,
Put his wife Draupadi at stake, feeling grim.

Once again, Duryodhana won, to his delight;
The enslaved Pandavas looked a sorry sight.

A guard went to fetch Draupadi, who was now a maid;
Draupadi sent him back, but she was very afraid.

Duryodhana sent Dushasana who dragged her by her hair;
Draupadi screamed and shrieked in utter despair.

'Maid, come and sit on my thigh!' Duryodhana cried;
'Never!' shouted Draupadi, and her tears dried!

Karna, already rejected by Draupadi, was also there;
He could have won her earlier, fair and square.

'A woman with five husbands is not a woman at all,'
Karna said, sounding malicious and small.

'A woman like her is a sheer disgrace;
She should be disrobed and shown her actual place!'

'Yes!' Duryodhana said, sounding quite pleased,
This chance to embarrass Draupadi, he quickly seized.

'Dushasana! remove all her clothes,' Duryodhana commanded;
'I want to embarrass her for insulting me,' he demanded.

Bhishma, Vidura and Arjuna asked the King to stop this act;
They said, 'She is your daughter-in-law, don't ignore this fact.'

Arjuna vowed to kill Karna for insulting Draupadi;
Duryodhana said, 'Stay quiet! You now have no authority.'

Draupadi, in despair, to Lord Krishna did pray;
She begged him to protect her on this mournful day.

Krishna had listened to Draupadi's prayer;
He knew what was happening, he was fully aware!

He performed a miracle, Draupadi to defend;
The clothes she wore seemed to have no end.

Dushasana couldn't disrobe her, nor bring her to shame;
While Draupadi kept on chanting Lord Krishna's name.

Annoyed and tired, Dushasana finally fell;
While Draupadi wept and looked unwell.

A furious Bhima vowed, 'Dushasana, you better take care;
With your blood Draupadi shall someday wash her hair!'

Bhima also vowed to break Duryodhana's thigh
For insulting Draupadi, before letting him die.

Duryodhana, a wrathful Draupadi, was about to curse;
But then Gandhari entered, before things became worse.

Gandhari begged Draupadi to spare her son;
But what had happened could not be undone.

Just then, Vidura got up and yelled in agony,
'My King, in this dice game what do you see?

I see that the Kauravas have made many a mistake;
But how could the Pandavas put their wife at stake?

For letting this happen, we should all be full of shame;
Between brothers, this was supposed to be a friendly game.'

Dhritarashtra said, 'Vidura, you are right, this has gone too far!'
He turned to Draupadi who was ready to declare war.

'Draupadi, ask for anything you desire.'
Draupadi then replied, raising her head higher.

'I ask for my freedom, and that of my husbands' too.'
'For sure!' Dhritarashtra said, 'This is granted to you.

But for your terrible suffering, we all should pay;
I give you back all that you have lost today.'

Duryodhana couldn't believe it and was full of rage;
The Pandavas, dejected, with Draupadi, left the stage.

They went back to Indraprastha without any further delay;
Hastinapur would pay a heavy price for what happened that day!

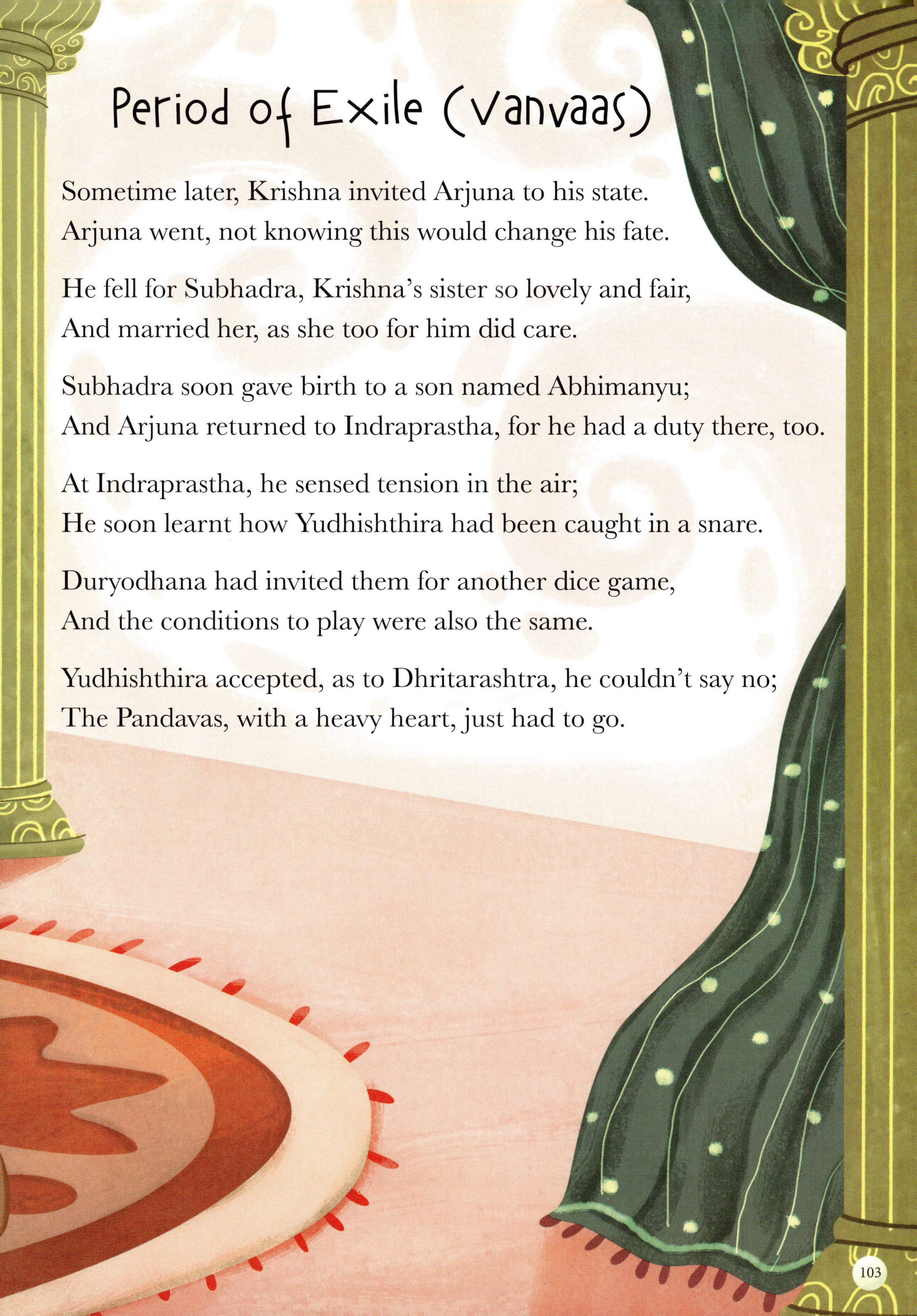

Period of Exile (vanvaas)

Sometime later, Krishna invited Arjuna to his state.
Arjuna went, not knowing this would change his fate.

He fell for Subhadra, Krishna's sister so lovely and fair,
And married her, as she too for him did care.

Subhadra soon gave birth to a son named Abhimanyu;
And Arjuna returned to Indraprastha, for he had a duty there, too.

At Indraprastha, he sensed tension in the air;
He soon learnt how Yudhishthira had been caught in a snare.

Duryodhana had invited them for another dice game,
And the conditions to play were also the same.

Yudhishthira accepted, as to Dhritarashtra, he couldn't say no;
The Pandavas, with a heavy heart, just had to go.

In the game, history repeated itself and the Pandavas lost,
But this time they had to a pay a slightly lower cost.

They had to spend twelve long years in a forest, a Vanvaas,
Followed by a year in disguise, which would be Agyatvaas.

If recognised during the Agyatvaas, they'd again have to hide;
The Pandavas were disheartened, but were compelled to abide.

Bhishma and the elders shook their heads in despair;
This win, like the earlier one, was very unfair!

The next day, in simple, white clothes the Pandavas came;
Yudhishthira was full of regret for playing the dice game.

Then the Pandavas sought blessings from everyone;
With Draupadi they left, to pay for what they'd done.

They built a hut in the forest and lived a simple life;
They weren't sorry for themselves, but for their delicate wife.

Draupadi, born a princess, did not deserve such a fate;
Yudhishthira was remorseful for his actions, but now it was too late.

Years passed by, and Duryodhana started to worry,
'Why did time have to go by in such a hurry?'

Shakuni sensed his worry, and crafted a new plan;
He was the most evil, wicked and malicious man.

He called Sage Durvasa, a very prominent sage,
Who always had a curse ready, and was mostly full of rage.

Duryodhana served the sage well, and then bid him adieu;
And then asked him to go and bless the Pandava brothers too.

Duryodhana knew that the Pandavas had nothing in their purse;
This would enrage Durvasa, he would throw on them a curse.

On seeing Sage Durvasa, the Pandavas were very glad;
But suddenly they realised, that no more food they had.

Only one more grain of rice, Draupadi could somehow find;
She knew that a hungry Sage Durvasa, would be very unkind.

'Help me, Krishna,' she prayed, and suddenly he did appear;
And saw a frightened Draupadi wiping off a tear.

'What's going on?' he said, 'I am famished and hungry.
Please, won't you go and bring some tasty food for me?'

'I only have this one grain of rice,'
Said Draupadi, and asked Krishna for advice.

Krishna ate the grain and the sage, feeling full, went happily away!
With this glorious miracle, Krishna had saved the day.

Krishna told the Pandavas that they should prepare for an attack;
They would have to go to war if they did not get Indraprastha back.

He then told Arjuna that thirteen years would soon pass by;
In a war against Bhishma and Dronacharya, the Pandavas would die.

He told him to pray hard to Lord Indra for his very special weapons,
Which could be obtained from nowhere else, but only from the heavens.

After months and months of praying, Lord Indra finally came;
He asked, 'What is the matter? Why did you chant my name?'

On being told, he said, 'Arjuna, to enter heaven, you must
First get Lord Shiva's permission, and his total trust.'

Arjuna prayed to Lord Shiva who a few months later did appear;
He blessed him to go to heaven, and asked him to be sincere.

Arjuna reached heaven, and soon started to learn;
One by one all Divya-astras, he was able to earn.

From the Apsaras, Arjuna learnt to dance and sing;
One of them named Urvashi, taught him everything.

She fell in love with Arjuna, and asked him for his hand;
Arjuna refused, hoping that she would understand!

Urvashi angrily cursed him to turn into a eunuch;
He couldn't remain a normal man, for him this was bad luck.

Indra said angrily, 'Urvashi! This curse you must reduce!'
Urvashi agreed, and she and Arjuna finally reached a truce.

Arjuna would have to be a eunuch for any one year of his choice.
'Use this curse during Agyatvaas,' Indra said in a commanding voice.

With heavenly weapons and a curse, to Earth, Arjuna returned;
He met his brothers and showed them all that he had earned.

The Pandavas continued to live a simple life in the forest;
They had almost completed twelve years of their test.

Dushala's husband, Jaidratha, was passing by, one day;
On seeing Draupadi, he tried to capture, and carry her away.

'Help! Help!' shrieked Draupadi and Arjuna and Bhima heard her cry;
They soon rescued Draupadi, and wanted Jaidratha to die.

They took him to Yudhishthira, who then righteously said,
'We shouldn't kill our brother-in-law, just shave off his head.'

Jaidratha, feeling ashamed, left with a vow to avenge;
The Pandavas now had another enemy, who wanted revenge.

The Pandavas' twelve years of exile were now nearly done;
The fate of Hastinapur now depended on the thirteenth one!

Year of Disguise (Agyatvaas)

The Pandavas looked for a place which was safe and sound;
It was time for Agyatvaas where they should not be found.

From Duryodhana's clever spies, they barely managed to escape;
By the time they passed through a forest, they were in a bad shape.

Yudhishthira asked Sahadeva to get water from a lake,
While the others rested to take a small break.

Reaching the lake, Sahadeva took some water in his hand;
He heard a voice, but from where it came, he could not understand.

It said, 'Answer my questions, before you drink!'
But Sahadeva drank anyway, he did not stop to think.

He died. And after him, so did Nakula, Arjuna and Bhima;
There is something wrong with the lake, to Yudhishthira it did seem.

Yudhishthira came and saw his brothers lying dead upon the ground;
'Who did this?' he shouted, as no one was around.

'I am Yaksha,' said a man who from nowhere did appear;
'I had warned them all before they drank and made my wishes clear.

Now if you wish to drink the water too,
My list of questions you must go through.

Who is heavier than the Earth?' Yaksha did then ask;
'One's mother,' replied Yudhishthira, to complete the task.

'Who is higher than the heavens?' Yaksha asked this time;
'One's father,' replied Yudhishthira, sounding very fit and fine.

'What is faster than the wind?' was his next question;
'The mind,' replied Yudhishthira, without changing his expression.

'Which enemy is invincible?' Yaksha asked, then;
'Anger,' said Yudhishthira, which was true for all men.

'Who is truly happy in this world?' Yaksha finally asked;
'One without debts,' Yudhishthira said, and the test he passed.

'As you have answered my questions, I'll give you a boon;
You can choose any one brother, who will be alive very soon.'

'I choose Nakula,' Yudhishthira said, without taking a pause;
'Why not Arjuna, or even Bhima?' Yaksha asked the cause.

'I am son of Kunti, and Nakula is Madri's son;
I consider both these mothers are truly like one.

If I am alive, then Madri's son should also get to live.'
Yaksha was impressed, and all the Pandavas he did forgive.

The Pandavas now alive, rushed back to Draupadi,
Who was clearly very anxious, and wanted them to hurry.

The twelve years of exile were already over and done;
If they were found now, all their efforts would be undone!

In the kingdom of Matsya they hid, which lay somewhere nearby,
Where in complete disguise, they waited for time to fly.

As a minister called Kanka, Yudhishthira was employed;
He had to play dice with the king, which he very much enjoyed.

Bhima, who loved food, as Ballava, became a cook;
Nakula and Sahadeva were cowherds, where no one would ever look.

Arjuna had turned into Brihanilla, a eunuch, using his curse;
Princess Uttara learnt to dance from the best archer in the universe!

Draupadi, as Sarandhari, disguised as a maid began to serve the queen;
Despite her guise, she was still the loveliest woman ever seen.

Draupadi, even in her rags, had not lost her charms;
Kichaka, the queen's brother, wanted to take her in his arms.

He asked his sister to tell her maid to bring him some wine;
They would then elope, and everything would be fine!

Draupadi was sent, but Kichaka's evil intent she did realise;
She ran away from there, and wanted his demise.

She told Bhima who killed Kichaka in his bed;
In the morning, he was just found dead!

When Duryodhana heard, his excitement could be seen;
He was as happy as he could have ever been!

'Only five people in the world could have killed that man;
Bhishma, Dronacharya, Karna, Bhima, and me,' he began.

'Four of us didn't do it, so only Bhima could have done the deed;
Now we know where the Pandavas are,' he said with evil greed.

The kingdom of Matsya was already under attack,
And their king was in battle, he could not come back.

Duryodhana decided it was time to take the Pandavas down;
With Bhishma and the others, he left to attack their town.

Prince Uttar, the crown prince of that state
Knew that his father's army, in coming would be too late!

He decided to go and fight the Kuru army on his own;
It was his duty to defend his state and also the throne.

'But who will I take as my trusted charioteer?
Father has taken them all, there's no one here!'

'Brihanilla can drive a chariot,' Draupadi did suggest;
Uttar said, 'I can manage well with him, as I am the best!'

Brihanilla, with Prince Uttar immediately set out;
He would win, Uttar truly had no doubt!

He got a shock when the mighty Kuru army he saw;
Against warriors like those, he felt very young and raw!

An army so vast, Uttar saw, and quickly ran away;
Arjuna ran after him, and said, 'You will have to fight today!'

Then Arjuna got his weapons which were hidden in a tree;
Since the thirteenth year was done, he revealed his identity.

With Uttar as charioteer, Arjuna strung Gandiva, his great bow;
This was Arjuna, now it was clear, and everyone did know.

He shot an arrow of respect at Bhishma and Dronacharya's feet;
Except Bhishma, one by one all the warriors, he went on to defeat.

Bhishma recognised it was Arjuna, and decided not to fight;
He watched Arjuna take everyone down; it was a grand sight!

Arjuna unarmed the soldiers, and Duryodhana and Dushasana, too;
It was only with Karna, that he had difficulty going through.

He shot an arrow of sleeping gas and they all fell asleep;
He went back to the tree where all the weapons he did keep.

Meanwhile, the king came back, and shouted at the queen;
'How could our son go and face the strongest army ever seen?'

When his son returned victorious, he praised his valour and his might;
'My son has defeated the Kuru army!' he said with great delight.

Uttar explained, 'Father, it is not I who fought;
I could never defeat them as I had thought.

A warrior helped me, for he felt it was right,
But then he left immediately, after the great fight.'

The next day, all the Pandavas came out in their original form;
The king apologised, that to them, he had not been warm.

He offered Uttara, his daughter, to Arjuna, for saving his son's head;
Arjuna asked for her to be married to his son Abhimanyu, instead.

Uttara and Abhimanyu were married, while Krishna presided;
No one knew that Hastinapur's future was being decided.

Krishna as Messenger of Peace

Duryodhana claimed he found the Pandavas in their year of disguise;
'But you found them after Agyatvaas,' countered Bhishma, being wise.

The stubborn Duryodhana then said, 'Indraprastha I will not give;
The Pandavas should again go back to the forest to live.'

He sent a messenger to Matsya to convey his demand;
Arjuna prepared for war, waited only for Yudhishthira's command.

Yudhishthira and Krishna calmly presided;
War was the last option, they decided.

'Peace should always be our first choice,'
Said Krishna, without raising his voice.

It was agreed that Krishna as a peace messenger would go;
We gave Duryodhana every opportunity, the world should know.

When the elders heard that Krishna himself would arrive,
They told Duryodhana not to offend him, if he wanted to stay alive.

Duryodhana tried to welcome Krishna, and even offered him food;
But Krishna declined his invitation politely, without sounding rude.

At this, Duryodhana was again filled with rage;
'How can that cowherd have such courage?'

Just then Bhishma and Dronacharya came;
To convince Duryodhana was their only aim.

Bhishma said, 'You must agree to whatever Krishna shall say,
For each and every word of his will be right in every way.'

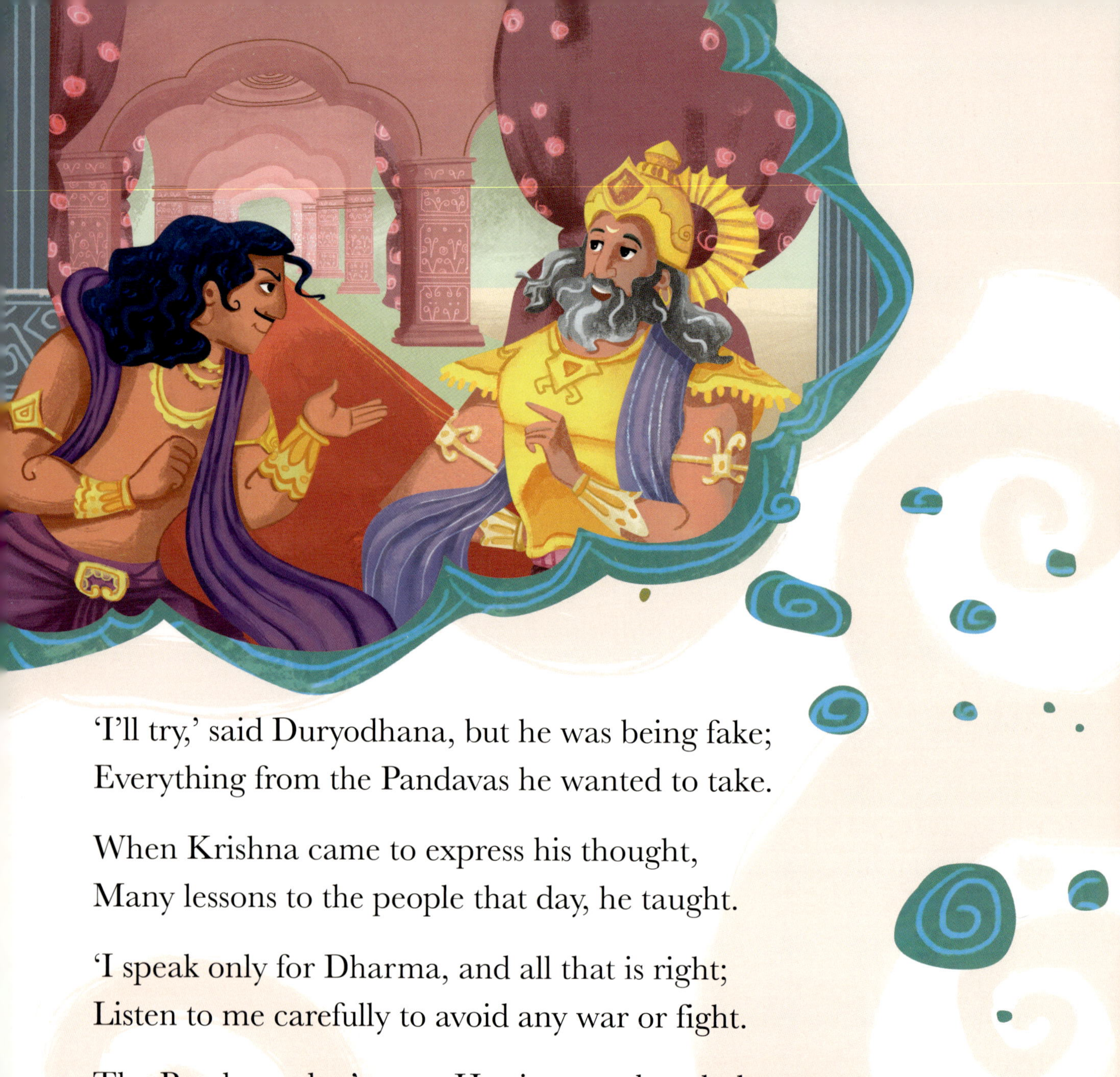

'I'll try,' said Duryodhana, but he was being fake;
Everything from the Pandavas he wanted to take.

When Krishna came to express his thought,
Many lessons to the people that day, he taught.

'I speak only for Dharma, and all that is right;
Listen to me carefully to avoid any war or fight.

The Pandavas don't want Hastinapur, the whole state;
They want peace and have asked me to negotiate.

Just give the Pandavas their Indraprastha back,
But do not think that the power to fight they lack.

Just give them Indraprastha, which is only half the state;
If you disagree, no one can protect you from your fate.'

'Never!' Duryodhana then firmly replied.
Even though he'd expected this, Krishna sighed.

'Then just give the Pandavas, five villages to stay.'
An enraged Duryodhana was in no mood to obey.

'I will not give the Pandavas a needle point of land!
Foolish cowherd, it is all mine, don't you understand?'

Said Duryodhana, which led to Krishna's temper being lost;
Duryodhana would now have to pay a very heavy cost!

'Duryodhana! you are on the path of self-destruction;
I gave you one last chance, but you ignored my instruction.

Now on your brothers' corpses you will weep;
Be it day or night, you will never sleep!

You have made wrong decisions, and you will fail;
Your poor mother on your corpses will sit and wail!'

'How dare you speak of my mother, you lowly cowherd?'
Duryodhana yelled, 'Enough of your nonsense I have heard!

If you say another word, I vow and I swear,
I will order you captured right then and there!'

'Ha-Ha Duryodhana,' Krishna laughed, 'Why don't you try?
If you want to capture me, first try to bind the sky!'

'Guards! Capture this cowherd,' Duryodhana demanded;
Everybody was shocked at what Duryodhana had commanded.

Hearing this, the Sudarshan came onto Krishna's right hand;
The aura of Krishna the court would now see and understand.

A blinding light appeared, and only the true-hearted ones could see,
Krishna in his actual form of Lord Vishnu, the One and Only!

Krishna grew bigger and bigger, and said finally,
'I am the Universe and the Universe is Me!

Duryodhana, you are blinded by power and have been fooled;
Hastinapur, happily you could have forever ruled.

Now there will be a war, and you will die!'
He left the assembly disappointed, though he did try.

But Krishna had not left Hastinapur just yet;
For Arjuna, there still remained a great threat!

Krishna knew that Karna was a better archer;
He had a secret to tell before his departure.

Karna came to Krishna for he had this to say,
'I want to apologise for Duryodhana's behaviour today.

A man should own up to his own mistake,
And responsibility for his actions he should take.'

'Karna, you are such a truthful and a good man,
How can you side with Duryodhana?' Krishna began.

'He is full of adharma, and a bad person too!'
Karna said, 'I know, Krishna, I agree with you.

But when the world betrayed me, only he gave me trust;
I cannot forget his kindness, repay him I must.'

Krishna said, 'Maybe, Duryodhana befriended you just for your skill,
For he knew that Arjuna only you would be able to kill.'

‘That may be so, but he stood by my side;
I will support him in war,’ Karna then replied.

Krishna sighed and solemnly said to Karna the most loyal,
‘Do you ever wonder if your mother is a royal?’

‘My mother is the one who raised me, and I will always be grateful;
She is the one who has taught me to be always faithful.’

‘I am talking about your real mother,’ Krishna said with a sigh;
Karna replied, ‘The one who floated me down a river, and left me to die?

I have thought about her and come to the conclusion,
That she must’ve been a princess who took this sad decision.

I must have been an accident which she didn’t want to show;
She gave me up, for she didn’t want the rest of the world to know.

She chose pride over a son who could have given her everything;
No praises for this kind of mother I shall ever think of, or sing.’

Krishna said, ‘Karna, you are right about your mother.
She now has sons, and you are their eldest brother.

Your mother has five more sons who can perform any feat;
They are invincible in war, and have never tasted defeat!'

'Five warriors,' Karna said slowly, 'who do you mean?'
'Yes, Karna,' Krishna smiled. 'Your mother is Kunti, the queen.

Why don't you leave Duryodhana, and be Indraprastha's king?
Your brothers will crown you gladly, and give you everything.'

Karna, devastated, said, 'I will have to fight my family;
Oh, what a terrible situation fate has given me!

But Krishna, you have to give me a vow;
My brothers should not know this now.

This is my destiny,' Karna then cried,
'I will never ever leave Duryodhana's side!'

Karna's loyalty towards Duryodhana would be remembered forever;
For Hastinapur, this war was inevitable, despite Krishna's endeavour.

Karna the Generous

Krishna was not the only one concerned;
For Karna's defeat, even Lord Indra yearned.

People would ask Karna for favours at sunrise,
Which he never refused, for he was generous and wise.

One night, while sleeping he had a dream;
It was a warning for his future, it did seem.

It said, 'Tomorrow Indra in disguise will come, so beware!
Don't give away your armour or earrings, or agony you'll bear.'

Karna was invincible till he wore his armour and earrings;
Indra was aware and wanted Karna to get rid of those things.

The next morning as said, Indra as an old lady came;
Karna, even though he knew, greeted her all the same.

'My boy, I am an old woman with a simple request;
Give me your earrings and the armour on your chest.'

Then Karna obliged, and cut them off from his body;
This sight shocked even Brahma, the Creator of everybody!

He gave them to Indra who could not bear to see,
Karna the generous, bleeding away in agony!

Indra said, 'Ask any boon from me!'
Karna wanted to vanquish his enemy.

He asked for the Vasavi Shakti, Indra's special weapon;
Indra was taken aback, he didn't expect this to happen.

But the boon he had to give as he'd promised him already;
Even though Karna could only use it once, he was now ready.

Karna thanked him, and to prepare for war, went back;
At Karna's generosity, even now, people are taken aback.

Meanwhile, Duryodhana and the Pandavas were getting ready for
The Mahabharata, which would be known as the greatest and holiest war!

Bhishma and Dronacharya had to take Hastinapur's side;
Only Vidura was free to choose, and he did decide.

'I support the Pandavas; and now I will leave.'
Dhritarashtra with sadness this news did receive.

Meanwhile, Shakuni realised the strength of his enemy,
So he sent Duryodhana to ask for Krishna's help and army.

Duryodhana reluctantly went to Krishna with this request;
Getting Krishna on their side would complete his quest.

Krishna was sleeping and Duryodhana took a seat;
Arjuna also entered and sat at Krishna's feet.

Krishna woke up and saw Arjuna first;
At this, Duryodhana had an outburst.

'Krishna, I had arrived much before,
Therefore, you should give me far more.'

'What do you both want?' Krishna asked with a sigh;
Each replied at the same time, 'I want you to be my ally.'

'I give an option,' Krishna said, 'for both of you to choose;
One of you can take the help of my Narayani army for your use.

The other one shall have just me, so decide what you wish to do,
For I won't use my weapons; now the choice is up to you.

Arjuna will choose first,' Krishna said, but Duryodhana did protest,
'I came first, so I should get to choose whatever is best.'

Krishna said, 'Arjuna is younger, so let him decide, it is only fair.'
'I only want you, Krishna,' Arjuna said with love and care.

'I want you to be my charioteer and guide me all the way.'
Krishna agreed immediately; and Arjuna had nothing else to say.

Duryodhana got the Narayani Sena, and was very, very pleased
With the fact that now, the strength of his army had increased.

War preparations on both sides had now begun;
Though there are many stories yet to be done.

Before the actual war began, Sage Veda Vyasa came to plead
That Dhritarashtra should convince Duryodhana to give up his greed.

A blind Dhritarashtra asked Sage Veda Vyasa to help him somehow see;
He wanted to know about the war, which would surely end in agony.

'I can grant you your sight!' but this proposal Dhritarashtra flatly refused;
'I want a live commentary of the war,' he said to Veda Vyasa who was confused.

Veda Vyasa then gave Sanjay, Dhritarashtra's charioteer, a special sight;
He would be able to see, and keep Dhritarashtra informed about the fight.

Meanwhile, Karna was lying down in bed;
Old memories were floating about in his head.

He remembered the days when at school,
To get knowledge, Sage Parashurama he did fool.

Parashurama would teach only a Brahmana,
For he considered that he would be a sinless one.

Karna, disguised as a Brahmana, had gone in his youth,
To learn skills that should only be earned with truth.

One day, while Sage Parashurama was taking a nap,
He unknowingly lay his head on Karna's lap.

An insect bit Karna, who bled, but stayed still;
All the pain he was able to handle due to his strong will.

A while later, when Sage Parashurama woke up, he saw
A pool of blood, which should have filled him with awe.

Instead, he shouted, 'Such pain, no Brahmana can withstand;
You are not a Brahmana, but a warrior, now I understand!

When your most important battle is being fought,
You will forget all the skills that I have taught.'

With this curse, he sent Karna away,
And Karna remembered it on this very day.

That morning, Kunti came with a favour to ask;
For her eldest son, she had a special task.

She wanted Karna to let all her sons live,
And herself, she wanted him to forgive.

Karna replied that he knew he was her son,
But the task she wanted couldn't be done.

'I will try to kill Arjuna as it is my fate;
But I can't send you back in this state.

The world knows you have five sons, and so it shall always be;
The gods will have to choose between Arjuna and me!'

Karna, by this promise, had spared the lives of his brothers;
He was the most generous man and he only lived for others.

War between Pandavas and Kauravas was now a certainty;
Hastinapur would be destroyed due to their enmity!

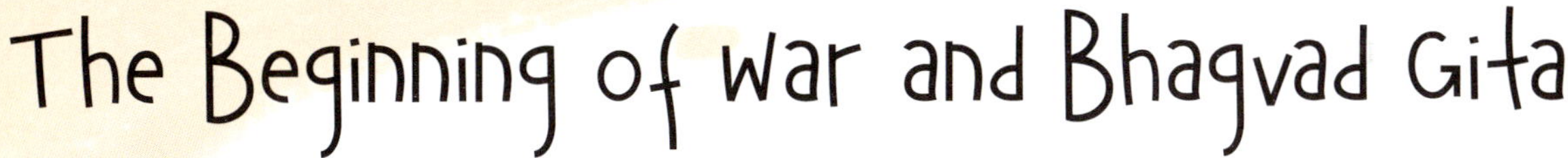

The Beginning of War and Bhagvad Gita

The armies were marching towards the ground;
This war would cause destruction for everyone around!

All the warriors were ready and looked at their rival;
Some would fight for victory, while others for survival.

Each warrior who was there had a definite goal;
Shikhandi was also there with Amba's soul.

Remember Amba? Who to kill Bhishma had taken a vow;
She was there in the form of Shikhandi, now.

After Bhishma's refusal to marry her, she wanted revenge;
Parashurama's aid she sought, her insult to avenge.

Parashurama called Bhishma and said, 'Amba you must marry!'
But Bhishma refused, as his oath he still had to carry.

'You must fight me,' Parashurama then did demand;
Bhishma said, 'I will do so as per your command.'

Bhishma, and his teacher Parashurama started to fight;
But both of them were equal in skill and might.

Parashurama then blessed Bhishma, raising both his hands;
And declared Bhishma the most powerful warrior in all the lands.

A hurt and angry Amba, prayed to Lord Shiva, and got a boon;
She would take the body of Shikhandi and be born again soon.

Shikhandi would be the cause of Bhishma's death,
And ensure that, in Kurukshetra, he took his last breath.

The Pandavas were led by Dhrishtadyumna, Draupadi's twin,
While the Kauravas would fight under Bhishma, to try and win.

The rules of war, Bhishma did decide;
By these rules, both the sides were to abide.

Knowing that Karna and the Pandavas had the same mother,
Bhishma couldn't let them fight, a brother against his brother!

Bhishma said, 'After deep thought, I had to decide,
That Karna will not fight from the Kauravas' side.'

Duryodhana was upset, but he had no choice;
Before Bhishma, no one could raise their voice.

Bhishma declared, 'I shall not kill anyone from the Kuru clan!'
How will we win this war? an alarmed Duryodhana wondered at this plan.

The conches blew and the armies marched forward;
No one wanted to lose or be seen as a coward.

The Pandavas' seven armies got into formation,
While the Kauravas' eleven armies stood in anticipation.

Yudhishthira went to Bhishma before the war could begin;
Bhishma blessed him and said, 'Do the best you can to win.'

Duryodhana, who was already upset, created a din,
But Bhishma said, 'I wish the best for all my kin.'

Yudhishthira went back, and said loudly,
'I hope everyone can listen to me!

Before Pitamaha Bhishma blows the conch for the war to start,
You all are free to change sides, without any guilt in your heart.'

Yuyutsu, Duryodhana's only step-brother, this opportunity did use;
He left Duryodhana, and Yudhishthira's side he did choose.

The main conch blew and thus began day one;
Many would be dead before the setting of the sun.

As Krishna drove the chariot, Arjuna suddenly wanted to stop the war;
He felt it was very wrong and said, 'What are we fighting for?'

He started crying, and with tearful eyes, he said,
'Krishna, just for a piece of land, all these people will soon be dead!'

Krishna froze time, and took his divine form to explain
The whole of Bhagwad Gita, to help Arjuna handle his pain.

He said, 'They were created for a purpose by God,
And questioning it would just be wrong and odd.

It is your duty to fight as a warrior, so do not sin;
Pick up your weapons and let this war begin.

Forget everything and fulfil your Dharma, your duty!'
'But how, Krishna?' Arjuna said, 'Please enlighten me.'

Krishna then went on to explain to him the deep meaning of life;
And what he should do and how, to overcome this inner strife.

Krishna said, 'Change is the law of the Universe;
Man is made by his beliefs, for better or for worse.

Hell has three gates, namely lust, anger and greed;
One should stay away from them, and always do good deeds.

Life is full of ups and downs, a balance you should maintain;
The death of your loved ones should not give you any pain.

For since the soul was never born, it cannot ever be dead;
Only the body gets worn, like clothes, and can therefore, be shed.

You were born on Earth, and will leave empty-handed, so please do not cry;
A person can only rise through his own mind, so he must try.

Wisdom becomes clouded when you have a selfish attitude;
Fear not, help will always come if you have gratitude.

Of everything I am the Beginning, the Middle and the End.'
Arjuna understood, and looked in awe at his divine friend.

'Krishna, I will do my duty and I will fight.'
Krishna disappeared into a ball of light.

He came back to his human form and unfroze time;
Arjuna fought valiantly, punishing the Kauravas for their crime.

Krishna taught mankind the gist of life and death;
Hastinapur and The Gita would be mentioned in the same breath.

Bhishma on His Deathbed

Day one ended with the Kauravas ahead;
They were strong as by Bhishma himself they were led.

A fearsome fighting took place on the second day;
Arjuna fought bravely till Bhishma came his way.

He remembered how he had sat on his lap;
Oh! Could this war have been a mishap?

Arjuna fought, but with less energy;
He was not really fighting for victory.

Krishna got up, and in anger raised his voice;
'Arjuna, I will break my vow, I now have no choice!'

Even though Krishna had vowed not to fight,
His weapon Sudharshan came onto his right.

'I will be honoured and lucky to be killed by you,'
Bhishma said, putting down his weapons too.

Arjuna said, 'No, Krishna! do not dishonour my name;
If you break your vow because of me, it will bring me shame.'

Krishna then put his Sudarshan away,
And Arjuna fought very well that day.

But nothing was enough to beat
The warrior that no one could defeat!

'What will we do?' Dhrishtadyumna loudly cried,
'To defeat Bhishma, all our warriors have tried!'

Bhishma continued to kill ten thousand soldiers each day;
He was invincible and no one could stand in his way.

It was already nine days since the war had begun,
Bhishma alone could ensure that the Kaurava army won.

The Pandavas were worried, despite being strong and brave;
They looked to Krishna to help them solve this problem so grave.

Krishna said, 'Fear not, just continue to fight,
And go and meet Bhishma in his tent tonight.'

They went and Bhishma blessed them with victory;
Arjuna said, 'Pitamaha, do not do this to me!

This blessing we cannot take from you,
As we are unable to make it come true.

We cannot win with you in our way!'
This is what Krishna had told them to say.

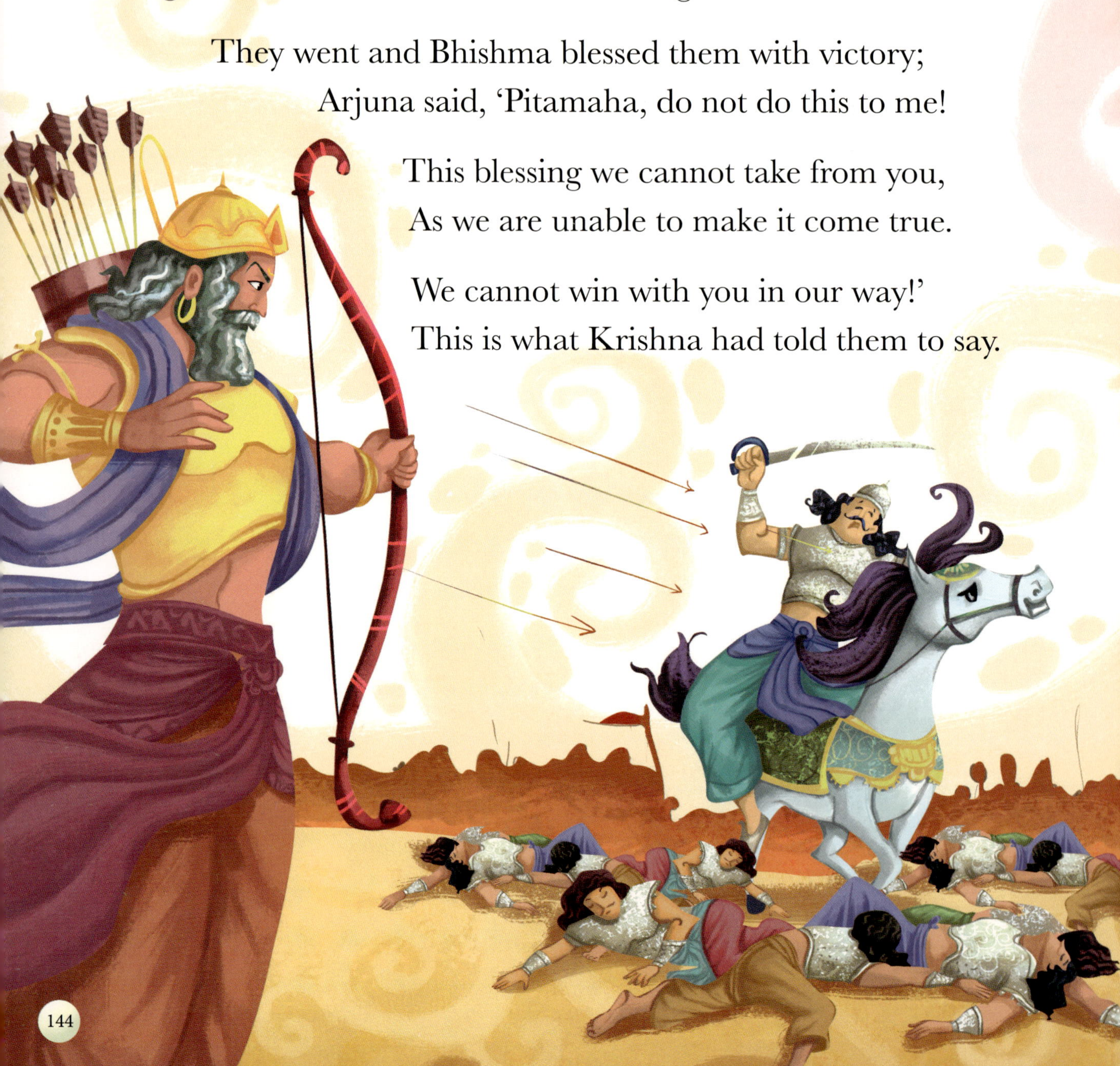

Bhishma said, 'I cannot take my blessing back;
Put a woman on your chariot and then attack!

As per rules, fighting a woman would not be right;
This is the only way to defeat me, as then I will not fight.'

When Krishna heard, he said, 'Now we have a solution.'
'How can we put a woman there?' asked Arjuna in confusion.

'We won't! Shikhandi will ride on your chariot, because
He is a man,' said Krishna. 'And it won't even break the laws.'

Arjuna asked, 'Why will Bhishma not fight this man?'
Krishna then went on to explain his grand plan.

'For Bhishma, Shikhandi is a woman in disguise;
He is actually Amba reborn to cause Bhishma's demise.'

The next morning, Bhishma went out for a walk;
When he saw Ganga, his mother, he stopped to talk.

He asked her, 'Why are you watering this piece of land?'
She replied, 'My son, you know everything and understand;

This spot will be your final resting place.'
'Ah!' said Bhishma with a smile on his face.

'I have been wondering what my life has been worth,'
Ganga replied, 'You have only lived for others since birth.'

Bhishma said, 'I have repaid all my debts, except one;
Amba's debt will be paid when this day is done.'

This tenth day of war no one would ever forget;
Bhishma would be on his deathbed by sunset!

Shikhandi stood on Arjuna's chariot that day;
They deliberately came in Bhishma's way.

Bhishma recognised Amba and put down his mighty bow;
He knew at once that it was finally his time to go.

As Arjuna shot his arrow, his tears he could not hold;
Bhishma was relieved as now he was tired and old.

Arjuna shot hundreds of arrows until Bhishma finally fell;
Despite all this pain and agony, he bravely smiled as well.

All the warriors came in front of him and all of them were blessed;
The greatest warrior was on his deathbed, but not at all depressed.

Arjuna could not control himself, his face was drenched in tears;
Bhishma blessed and thanked him, for relieving him after all these years.

Devavrata, renamed Bhishma, from the age of sixteen,
Was the most accomplished warrior the world had ever seen!

Now resting on a bed of arrows waiting for the end of his days;
That piece of land was blessed, on which the greatest warrior lay.

Krishna, Lord Vishnu himself, went up to Bhishma to pay his respect;
That Bhishma lay on his deathbed was difficult to accept.

This war had caused its biggest casualty with this act of violence;
Hastinapur would never be the same without Bhishma's grand presence.

Arjuna Avenges Abhimanyu's Death

The Pandavas, though upset, felt a sense of relief;
Duryodhana furious, begged Dronacharya to be their new chief.

Day eleven began and the armies continued their fight;
Karna too was allowed in the battlefield to prove his might.

Even after the sun had set, Duryodhana's armies did not stop;
By defying the rules, his armies stayed at the top.

The greatly weakened Pandava army had nearly lost the game;
So they were very relieved when Bhima's son Ghatotkacha came.

Ghatotkacha to the Pandava army, a new vigour gave;
It was well known to all that he was strong and brave.

He was huge in size and so, the Kaurava army was scared;
To prevent damage to his army, Duryodhana then declared:

'I close the fight for this eleventh day!'
For he wanted to get this demon out of the way.

The next day, Ghatotkacha tore apart each enemy he did meet;
The frightened Kaurava army, could clearly sense defeat.

When Ghatotkacha turned towards him, Duryodhana gave out a cry;
'Karna, do save me, otherwise he'll cause me to die.

Please kill this half-demon with Indra's weapon now.'
Duryodhana begged Karna, to save him any how.

'This weapon is saved to kill Arjuna,' Karna then said;
Duryodhana cried, 'What will be the point if I'm already dead?'

Karna was compelled to use the divine weapon,
And thus killed Ghatotkacha who was Bhima's mightiest son.

The Pandavas were upset, but Krishna was relieved;
Arjuna was now saved, and Ghatotkacha had done his deed.

Duryodhana, realising the situation, now made a plan;
He then went up to Dronacharya and cunningly began.

'I want Yudhishthira captured,' he curtly demanded;
'You are a great warrior and can do this single-handed!

I regard them as my brothers, whom I don't want to kill;
When Hastinapur is all mine, I can utilise their skill!'

Dronacharya was convinced by Duryodhana's good intent;
The thirteenth day of the war could prove to be a great event.

The special war formation, the Chakravyuha, Dronacharya did plan;
Which only Arjuna and Krishna could break, in the whole of their clan.

Duryodhana sent the Trigarta brothers to distract Arjuna for long;
They would not be defeated easily, as they were very strong.

The Pandavas, with Arjuna and Krishna away, were filled with concern;
As Duryodhana could win the war that day, with this one turn.

Arjuna's son Abhimanyu then came out;
'I know how to get in,' he said with a shout!

'My father had told my mother when I was in the womb;
He had explained about Chakravyuha to her in her room.

He had told her how to get inside,
But before he told her how to get outside,

My mother, not interested, had gone off to sleep;
So getting inside is the only information I could keep.'

'We will figure it out,' Yudhishthira said casually,
'Now how to get inside child, please do tell me.'

They crossed the first round and Yudhishthira cried,
'Proceed Abhimanyu, I will stay by your side.'

Abhimanyu then managed to enter the second round,
But he could only hear Duryodhana's warriors around.

Jaidratha had stopped Yudhishthira and the others,
For, after being insulted by the Pandava brothers,

He had prayed to Lord Shiva who had appeared soon,
And granted Jaidratha a specially desired boon.

'Jaidratha, for one day only, you'll be able to perform this feat;
Except Arjuna, all the Pandavas you will be able to defeat!'

Today was the day to fulfil that request;
Abhimanyu was left alone in his quest.

All the Kaurava warriors together killed Abhimanyu, fighting as one;
By doing wrong and disobeying Bhishma's rules, the Kauravas had won.

Abhimanyu, Krishna's disciple, fought bravely but was defeated;
The Pandavas were angry, because the Kauravas had cheated.

Arjuna heard the news when he came;
Jaidratha was the one he chose to blame.

He vowed to kill Jaidratha by sunset the next day,
Or else he would jump in the fire and give his life away!

The fourteenth day began with Arjuna full of fire;
He wanted to send Jaidratha to his funeral pyre.

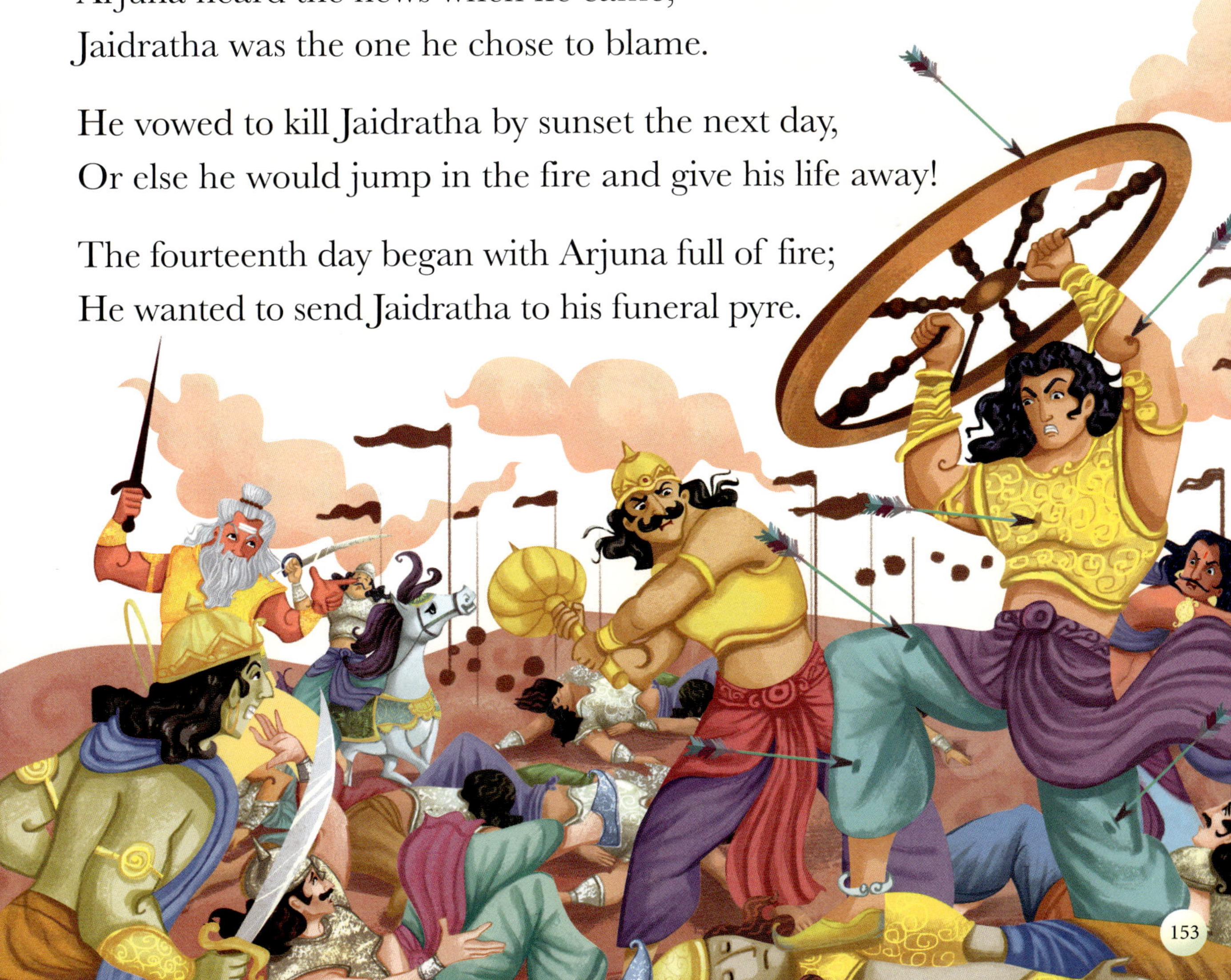

'Jaidratha!' he screamed, 'Don't hide;
I will kill you, Oh! Jaidratha, come outside!'

The Kauravas had heard Arjuna's vow;
They had a chance to kill Arjuna now.

Arjuna fought each warrior but could not find
Jaidratha, who was protected by the army, and hiding behind.

Krishna, who worried about Arjuna, was not amused;
He then did something that made Jaidratha confused.

With his powers Krishna hid the sun, making it dark;
Jaidratha laughed, and came outside, lighting a spark.

He said, 'Arjuna, now who should jump into the fire?
It is time for you to leave this world and retire.'

Krishna revealed the sun and said,
'Quick, Arjuna! strike this evil man dead.

But remember, don't let his head fall on the floor,
For Jaidratha has protections even when he is no more.

He has a boon that whoever makes his head fall on the ground,
Will be killed instantly, without hearing another sound.

Send his head to his father, who is resting in the mountain range;
He deserves to die for giving Jaidratha this boon that is so strange.'

Arjuna did so, and all of the Pandavas cheered;
Duryodhana raged, it was what he had secretly feared.

Arjuna had fulfilled his vow as Jaidratha was now dead;
But Hastinapur's future was still hanging by a thread

Duryodhana Left Alone in the Battlefield

The Pandavas were now worried about their guru;
How to defeat Dronacharya, they simply had no clue.

They went to Krishna to seek his advice,
Who told them a way to bring about his demise.

An elephant was named Ashwatthama, same as Dronacharya's son;
Krishna asked Bhima to kill the elephant, so the war could be won.

Bhima did as advised, and triumphantly said,
'I have killed Ashwatthama! Now Ashwatthama is dead!'

'Is Ashwatthama really dead?' Dronacharya asked, to which Yudhishthira replied,
'Yes, he is!' and so, for the first time the truthful and honest Yudhishthira lied.

He said softly, 'Ashwatthama the elephant, not the man has died.'
But Dronacharya did not hear it, his grief he could not hide.

He sat down with tearful eyes, and Dhrishtadyumna cut off his head;
Before anyone could realise, Dronacharya the great was dead!

When Ashwatthama got to know, he wanted to pay the Pandavas back;
But he controlled his anger, and waited for the right time to attack.

The Pandavas were disturbed, but heaved a sigh of relief;
An angry Duryodhana then declared Karna as the next chief.

Yudhishthira being a Dharmaraj used to have his chariot in the air,
For he was considered the most righteous, just and fair.

When he told this lie, his chariot at once returned to the ground;
His image of being honest and truthful forever had been drowned.

Dhrishtadyumna was not the only one to do what had been planned;
At the same time, Dushasana too had been killed at Bhima's hand.

Bhima drank the blood from his chest, which he did tear;
He then took some blood for Drapaudi to wash her hair.

Draupadi washed her hair with his blood to her satisfaction;
Duryodhana was furious, and also sad, at Bhima's cruel action.

The fifteenth day of war ended with great loss on the Kauravas' side;
All their hopes now rested on Karna to turn the tide.

On the sixteenth day, Karna and Arjuna did come face to face;
Arjuna said, 'Charioteer's son! Today I'll show you your real place.'

Then Karna took out a magical arrow and took aim;
Krishna knew that Arjuna won't be able to handle the same.

Krishna, using his divine powers, pushed Arjuna's chariot down;
Karna's arrow missed Arjuna's head and only hit his crown.

Krishna had saved Arjuna from another fatal threat;
But Karna the warrior was not ready to give up yet.

Karna's next arrow would disarm Arjuna, and victory he would get;
But a second before he shot, he realised that the sun had set.

Karna said, 'The sun has saved you today,
But tomorrow I will definitely have my way.'

Duryodhana asked Karna, 'What have you done?
If you had killed Arjuna, we would have won.

So what if the sun had set, we've broken the rules before;
No one would have questioned us if we had done it once more.'

Karna replied, 'While I am commander of this army,
Nobody can break Bhishma's rules, not even me!'

The seventeenth day began with Karna leading the way;
Before fighting Arjuna, he fought the other Pandavas that day.

He could have killed them all, and put them to eternal sleep,
But his promise to his mother Kunti he had to keep.

'Your five sons will live,' he kept these words in his mind;
He spared their lives, and then Arjuna he went to find.

The time had now come for their final fight;
Both the warriors were ready to show off their might.

Arjuna's arrow struck Karna's chariot and moved it ten steps back;
Arjuna's chariot moved back, only two steps on Karna's attack.

Krishna was surprised and praised Karna no end;
Arjuna was confused, and questioned his friend.

Krishna reminded Arjuna that he himself was sitting there;
As Lord, he had the weight of the Universe, land, water and air.

In these two days, Karna had already shown his mettle;
He had proved all his worth, there was no score left to settle.

But things changed, and Karna's chariot wheel got stuck;
He got down to fix it and Krishna told Arjuna to try his luck.

Arjuna said, 'It's against the rules of war to kill him right now!'
But Krishna said, 'This is your best chance to complete your vow.'

Arjuna was reluctant, but still raised his bow and arrow;
Seeing it, his strongest weapon, Karna wanted to show.

But just then, Sage Parashurama's curse did set in;
Karna forgot his skills, and could do nothing to win.

Arjuna took aim and stuck Karna with all his might and force;
Karna could only watch and was now filled with remorse.

He shouted out at Arjuna for attacking him in this way;
He had expected better from Arjuna even on this day.

Karna was the best archer in the world to ever live;
He was the most generous person, for everything he did give.

Karna's death was a sad and devastating event;
The Pandavas, to win this war, would go to any extent.

Meanwhile, Sahadeva killed Shakuni with all his skill;
Duryodhana had lost everything, even his will.

He had nobody left, no friend by his side;
That night, he went to Bhishma and cried.

'My friend Karna, the only person I cared about, is dead!
What should I live for? Someone should put me on my death bed!'

Bhishma said, 'Duryodhana, you were lucky to have a friend so loyal;
He stayed true to you even though his mother was a royal.'

Duryodhana stopped crying and asked, 'Who is his mother?'
Bhishma replied, 'You know her as Kunti, the queen and no other.'

'You mean those Pandavas are Karna's brothers?' Duryodhana asked;
'Yes,' replied Bhishma, 'And Karna was aware of his past.'

'I will never have such a friend,' Duryodhana did claim,
'For without Karna, my life will never be the same!'

Meanwhile, Kunti walked on to the battlefield;
Her tears she tried really hard to shield.

She went to Karna's corpse and bitterly cried;
Her eldest and most unfortunate son, had died!

The Pandavas came and looked at their mother;
'Why are you crying for this charioteer's son?' they asked her.

Kunti replied, 'He is mine, and not a charioteer's son!'
Yudhishthira was shocked and said, 'Mother, what have you done?

You have made us kill our own elder brother!
You could have stopped this war anytime, mother!

Before the war, this truth you should have spoken!'
The Pandavas were very sad, and heartbroken.

Angry at Kunti's lie, Yudhishthira cursed the whole of womankind;
That none of them would ever be able to keep a secret in their mind.

Sage Parashurama's three great disciples were now out of the battle.
Duryodhana was left alone amidst a silence that made him rattle.

He had lost all ninety-nine of his brothers as well;
For Hastinapur, was it worth it? Only time would tell.

Everything Lost, Nothing Gained

That night, Duryodhana went to meet Gandhari,
To seek his mother's blessings for victory.

'I cannot grant you this wish,' she said,
'But I can give you something else instead.'

She asked him to bathe and come back undressed;
Duryodhana was unable to understand and was not impressed.

But he still carried out her wish, and after his bath,
He saw Krishna standing in his path.

He quickly covered his thighs with his hand;
Krishna knew what Gandhari had planned.

'Oh, Duryodhana!' he cried, 'You are now a grown person;
You cannot go to Gandhari naked, despite being her son.'

Duryodhana was ashamed, so he took Krishna's advice,
Not knowing that for this he would pay a heavy price.

He covered his thighs with a bamboo leaf,
And went to meet his mother with a sigh of relief.

Gandhari said to him, 'My son, today,
After years of penance, a chant I shall say.

I will now open my blindfold to see,
My precious first-born son standing in front of me.

I will make your body as hard as stone;
No one will be able to break a single bone.'

With that, she finally opened her eyes,
And saw that her son had been unwise.

She said, 'Why didn't you follow my instruction?
You have left an opportunity for your destruction.

Now, except your thighs, you are hard as stone;
Oh, why did you act so foolishly on your own?'

The eighteenth day of war began, but Duryodhana was not there;
A messenger told Yudhishthira that for war, Duryodhana did not care.

The Pandavas looked for him, and saw him resting by a lake;
Bhima declared, 'Duryodhana, it's time to pay for your mistake!'

Duryodhana replied, walking towards them with a sad face,
'Keep Hastinapur, I no longer want to fight for any place.'

Yudhishthira raged, 'We have come so far,
Now we will kill you and will win this war!'

Duryodhana shouted back, 'I will fight and win,
Unlike you, Pandavas, I will not commit a sin.'

Bhima and Duryodhana then fought with a mace;
Bhima tried hard but Duryodhana was like a stone at every place.

They fought valiantly, and tirelessly, for a very long while;
Bhima, afraid of losing, looked at Krishna who wore a smile.

He asked Bhima to attack Duryodhana's thighs;
Bhima was confused, but listened to Krishna's advice.

To hit under the waist, the rules of war did not allow;
But it was the only way for Bhima to win and complete his vow.

He hit him really hard; with a cry Duryodhana went down;
The Pandavas had broken the rules of war to win this crown.

Duryodhana was helpless and the Pandavas left him there to die;
Dronacharya's son Ashwatthama then came to say goodbye.

Duryodhana appointed him as chief and said with his dying breath,
'Give the cheating Pandavas the punishment of death.'

Duryodhana's death meant that the war had officially ended;
The Pandavas had achieved what they had intended.

That night with everyone sleeping, Ashwatthama sought revenge;
He killed Dhrishtadyumna, his father's death he was able to avenge.

Mistaking them for the Pandavas, he killed five warriors in their bed,
Not realising that he had killed Draupadi's five sons instead!

When Draupadi heard about the death of her brother and her sons,
She wanted Ashwatthama to pay for the death of her dear ones.

Meanwhile, as Ashwatthama found out about his mistake,
He went to a sage as amends he truly wanted to make.

But when he saw the Pandavas looking for him,
He could not control himself, as he was feeling grim.

He took out the Brahmastra weapon, and loudly did scream,
'Your clan's future will now remain an unfulfilled dream.

I can't kill you, but I will kill your descendant
On whom your entire future is dependent.'

Then Ashwatthama shot an arrow into Uttara's womb;
Arjuna's unborn grandson, Parikshit, now faced doom.

Krishna cursed Ashwatthama for this dreadful deed;
He would suffer and live forever, and never be freed.

Krishna then went up to Parikshit, who was lying dead and still;
With his divine powers, he gave him life as per his will.

He blessed Parikshit to rule Hastinapur for many years to come;
The Pandavas then went to Bhishma to tell him the outcome.

Bhishma was now relieved that Hastinapur was safe and sound;
He could die peacefully, Hastinapur no longer needed him around.

He then revealed to the Pandavas some vital facts of life;
About how things could have been different, with no war and no strife.

He started with his own mistake of taking that dreadful vow;
'I shouldn't have ever done that, when I think about it now.

Then it was Dhritarashtra's blind love towards his eldest son;
He should not have favoured him, considering what all he had done.

To cause this war, the evil Shakuni also played a major part;
Gandhari, if not blindfolded, could have changed things from the start.

Duryodhana himself could have very easily avoided the war;
His jealousy towards you, Pandavas, was totally uncalled for.

He could have ruled Hastinapur peacefully forever;
He should not have desired Indraprastha, ever!

Yudhishthira, you should never have played the dice game;
You should not have bet your wife as it brought you all to shame.

Draupadi should also have been calmer, and much more restrained;
If she hadn't insulted Duryodhana, so much could have been gained.

Kunti's eldest son, Karna, too, could have changed the tide,
If only he had switched over to his real brothers' side.'

Bhishma's words of wisdom were very carefully heard;
The Pandavas silently understood each and every word.

Devastated, they fell at Bhishma's feet and full of regret, cried;
Bhishma, the son of Ganga, closed his eyes and died.

With Bhishma's death, this epic tale is now done.
Everyone had lost and no one had actually won.

This story teaches us lessons to which we can all relate;
We should learn from Bhishma's life and Hastinapur's fate!

CHARACTERS AND PLACES

Chapter 1

1. Hastinapur - kingdom in ancient India
2. Shantanu - king of Hastinapur; husband of goddess Ganga and Satyawati
3. Ganga - a river personified as a goddess in ancient India
4. Devavrata - son of goddess Ganga and King Shantanu
5. Satyawati - second wife of King Shantanu
6. Bhishma - name given to Devavrata by his mother, goddess Ganga, after he took the vow of celibacy

Chapter 2

7. Chitrangada - elder son of Satyawati and King Shantanu
8. Vichitravirya - second son of Satyawati and King Shantanu
9. Kashi - kingdom in ancient India
10. Kashya - king of Kashi
11. Amba - eldest daughter of King Kashya who refused to marry Vichitravirya; reborn as Shikhandi
12. Ambika - second daughter of King Kashya; married to Vichitravirya; mother of Dhritarashtra
13. Ambalika - third daughter of King Kashya; married to Vichitravirya; mother of Pandu
14. Shalva - king in ancient India whom Amba wished to marry
15. Veda Vyasa - sage in ancient India
16. Dhritarashtra - blind son of Ambika and Sage Veda Vyasa; husband of Gandhari; patriarch of the Kaurava princes
17. Pandu - son of Ambalika and Sage Veda Vyasa; patriarch of the Pandava princes; husband of Kunti and Madri
18. Vidura - son of a maid of the queens of Hastinapur and Sage Veda Vyasa

Chapter 3

19. Subala - king of Gandhar, a kingdom in ancient India
20. Gandhari - daughter of King Subala; wife of Dhritarashtra; mother of the Kaurava princes
21. Shakuni - son of King Subala; brother of Gandhari
22. Surasena - king of Surasena, a kingdom in ancient India
23. Kunti - daughter of King Surasena; first wife of King Pandu; mother of the Pandavas-Yudhishthira (by Dharmaraj) Arjuna (by Indra) and Bhima (by Vayu)
24. Durvasa - sage in ancient India, known for his anger
25. Madra - king of Madra, kingdom in ancient India
26. Madri - sister of King Madra; second wife of King Pandu; co-wife to Kunti; mother of Nakula and Sahadeva by Ashwin twins

Chapter 4

27. Mantra - kingdom in ancient India
28. Kansa - evil king of Mathura kingdom
29. Vasudeva - son of King Surasena; brother of Kunti
30. Devaki - sister of King Kansa; wife of Vasudeva; mother of Lord Krishna
31. Rohini - other wife of Vasudeva; adoptive mother of Balarama
32. Nandagaon - village within kingdom of Mathura
33. Sheshnag - serpent god; reclining couch and canopy of Lord Vishnu
34. Vishnu - one of the three main gods forming the holy Hindu trinity
35. Nanda - head of Nandagaon; adoptive father of Lord Krishna
36. Yashoda - wife of Nanda; adoptive mother of Lord Krishna
37. Krishna - eighth son of Devaki and Vasudeva; reincarnation of Lord Vishnu
38. Makhan Chor - butter thief, as the child Krishna was fondly called
39. Balarama - seventh son of Devaki and Vasudeva; nurtured by Rohini
40. Gopis- female friends of Krishna in Nandagaon
41. Radha - a gopi in Nandagaon; dearest and constant companion of Lord Krishna
42. Kalia Naag - a multi-hooded, poisonous snake in river Yamuna as it flowed through Nandagaon; killed by Lord Krishna
43. Indra - Lord of heavens and rain

44. Govardhan - mountain near Nandagaon; Krishna lifted it on his finger to save people from Indra's wrath.
45. Shiva - one of the three main gods forming the holy Hindu trinity
46. Sandipani Ashram - hermitage of Sage Sandipani
47 Ugrasena - Krishna's grandfather who became king of Mathura after Kansa was killed.

Chapter 5

48. Dharmaraj - lord of truth and righteousness
49. Yudhishthira - firstborn son of Kunti (with Dharmaraj)
50. Vayu - wind god
51. Bhima - second son of Kunti (born from Vayu)
52. Arjuna - third son of Kunti (born from Indra)
53. Ashwin twins - sons of sun god Surya
54. Nakula - one of the twins born to Madri (from Ashwin twins)
55. Sahadeva - one of the twins born to Madri (from Ashwin twins)
56. Dushala - only daughter of Gandhari and King Dhritarashtra, wife of Jaidratha
57. Duryodhana - eldest son of Gandhari and King Dhritarashtra
58. Yuyutsu - son of Gandhari's maid and King Dhritarashtra
59. Adhiratha - charioteer of King Dhritarashtra
60. Karna - eldest son of Kunti (from sun god Surya); adopted son of Adhiratha
61 Sanjay - charioteer of King Dhritarashtra
62. Kauravas - combined name for the hundred sons of King Dhritarashtra
63. Pandavas - combined name for the five sons of King Pandu
64. Kripacharya - sage and family guru(teacher) of Hastinapur
65. Dronacharya - sage and brother-in-law of Kripacharya
66. Kuru princes - descendants of King Kuru / princes of Hastinapur (Kauravas and Pandavas)
67. Dushasana - second son of Gandhari and King Dhritarashtra
68. Nagas - a hardy and warlike tribe
69. Kuntibhoja - king of Nagas and adoptive father of Kunti
70. Eklavya - a tribal village boy in Hastinapur who excelled in archery
71. Gurudakshina - an offering to the guru (teacher)

Chapter 6

72. Rangabhoomi - an arena for performing arts and skills
73. Ashwatthama - son of Kripi and Sage Dronacharya
74. Parashurama - sage in ancient India and Guru(teacher) of Bhishma, Dronacharya and Karna
75. Anga - a princely state of Hastinapur

Chapter 7

76. Guru - teacher
77. Drupada - king of Panchala, a kingdom in ancient India
78. Kripi - wife of Sage Dronacharya; sister of Sage Kripacharya
79. Sandipani - sage in ancient India and Guru(teacher) of Krishna and Balarama
80. Sudarshan Chakra - weapon of Lord Vishnu

Chapter 8

81. Varnavrat - a town in Hastinapur

Chapter 9

82. Swayamvar- an ancient Indian practice in which a girl chooses a husband from a group of suitors.
83. Hidimbi - a female monster; sister of Hidimbasura; wife of Bhima
84. Draupadi - daughter of King Drupada; married to the five Pandava brothers
85. Shikhandi - eldest son of King Drupada; prince of Panchala
86. Dhrishtadyumna - second son of King Drupada; prince of Panchala

Chapter 10

87. Khandavprastha- barren, demons' land situated in Hastinapur
88. Maya- demon living in Khandavprastha
89. Indraprastha- rechristened name of Khandavprastha after the Pandavas turned it fertile with the help of Lord Indra

Chapter 11

90. Rajsuya Yagya - a ritual performed before the sacred fire
91. Jarasandha - king of Magadha, a kingdom in ancient India
92. Jara - a female monster
93. Brahmana - priest
94. Trigarta - kingdom in ancient India
95. Trigarta brothers - princes of Trigarta kingdom
96. Yagya - a ritual performed before the sacred fire

Chapter 13

97. Subhadra - daughter of Rohini and Vasudeva; sister of Lord Krishna and Balarama; wife of Arjuna, mother of Abhimanyu
98. Abhimanyu - son of Subhadra and Arjuna
99. Vanvaas - living in forest
100. Agyatvaas - living anonymously in disguise
101. Divya-astra - a divine weapon
102. Apsara - celestial nymph
103. Urvashi - an apsara
104. Jaidratha - husband of Dushala; brother-in-law of Duryodhana
105. Yaksha - a nature spirit
106. Matsya - kingdom in ancient India
107. Kanka - Yudhishthira's name in disguise during Agyatvaas
108. Ballava - Bhima's name in disguise during Agyatvaas
109. Brihanilla - Arjuna's name in disguise during Agyatvaas
110. Uttara - princess of Matsya kingdom; wife of Abhimanyu
111. Sarandhari - Draupadi's name in disguise during Agyatvaas
112. Kichaka - brother of queen of Matsya;killed by Bhima for harassing Draupadi
113. Uttar - prince of Matsya
114. Gandiva - Arjuna's special bow

Chapter 15

115. Adharma - Unrighteousness, evil

Chapter 16

116. Brahma - one of the three main gods forming the holy Hindu trinity
117. Vasavi Shakti - Indra's special invincible weapon
118. Mahabharata - the great war between the Pandavas and the Kauravas
119. Narayani army/sena - name of Krishna's army

Chapter 17

120. Kurukshetra - the battlefield of the Mahabharata
121. Bhagwad Gita - holy book of Hindu religion containing the teachings of Lord Krishna to Arjuna during the Mahabharata
122. Dharma - righteousness
123. Pitamaha - Grandfather

Chapter 19

124. Ghatotkacha - son of Hidimbi demon and Bhima
125. Chakravyuha - special war formation

Chapter 21

126. Brahmastra - special invincible weapon of Lord Brahma
127. Parikshit - son of Uttara and Abhimanyu

ACKNOWLEDGEMENTS

I would like to thank all the people who made this journey special for me:

My parents, who read to me when I was little, and who always supported and inspired me, and made me fall in love with this timeless epic;

My sister, Saisha, my biggest critic and greatest fan, who irritated me as much as I irritated her, and then loved me as much as any little sister can;

My grandparents, who sat and watched me, bewildered and amazed, as I retold the Mahabharata to them;

My teachers and friends, who tolerated a scatter-brained girl, who would occasionally spout poetry.

And my heartfelt thanks to the entire team at Om Books International:

Ajay Mago, Publisher, Om Books International, for giving a young 9-year-old girl the opportunity that changed her life;

Dr. Kirti Pathak, my erudite and patient editor, who taught me much about this epic and helped me to turn the 'uncut' book into a bright sparkling jewel;

Anshuman Pandey, Harish Arya and Savita Kundal, for bringing my words to life with their vibrant and beautiful illustrations;

Namita Gokhale, Shobhaa De, Subhadra Sen Gupta, Amitabh Kant, for all their encouragement;

And last but not least, thank you, dear readers, for picking up The Mahabharata in Rhyme. I hope my version of this epic tale delights and enlightens you.

ABOUT THE AUTHOR

Twelve-year-old Sia Gupta is currently studying in Grade 7 in Modern School, New Delhi. Deeply interested in poetry, Sia wrote her first book titled "The Magical World of Poems", at the age of 8. She wrote the "Tales in Rhyme" series based on the popular tales of "Aladdin", "Cinderella", "Snow White and the Seven Dwarfs" and "Beauty and the Beast" when she was 9 years old. The series won her the Federation of Indian Publishers Award. With a keen interest in Indian mythology, she wrote "The Mahabharata in Rhyme" at the age of ten. With a desire to spread the joy of reading and writing among her peers, she has presented "Ten Tips to Publish at Ten", a 45-minute interactive event, to grade 4 and 5 students across various schools. She is an avid reader and her favourite genres are epic poetry and fantasy fiction. Sia also plays the piano and loves to dance.